What Fretzin'

"Many in the legal marketing and business development space promise results. Steve Fretzin delivers. In his typical straightforward, honest, and cogent fashion, Steve once again provides valuable tips and advice on how to take your business development efforts and firm to the next level. This book is a must-read (and his podcast is a must-hear)."
Frank Ramos, Partner, Clarke Silvergate, P.A.

"Steve Fretzin continues to create amazing content for lawyers in a way that is digestible and practical to follow. What I love about this book is that it isn't big picture theory or ideology rather Steve delivers common sense tools lawyers can use to get real results."
Seth Price, Founder of BluShark Digital

"I don't have time to sit down and read a long-winded book (that should have been a blog post to start with) and try to figure out where the actionable items are buried in the book. Steve Fretzin does all the work for me and presents his insights and observations in bite-sized, easily read, direct and to the point valuable selections that deliver time and time again."
Neil Tyra, The Tyra Law Firm, LLC

"You'll find yourself nodding along in agreement as Fretzin drives home foundational business concepts through a familiar, accessible, almost folksy narrative. This book is equal parts business acumen, motivational insight and out-of-the box thinking."
Conrad Saam, Mockingbird

"One way to 'be that lawyer' is to leave your cat filter on in a Zoom meeting. However, the better way to 'be that lawyer' is to build a practice that other lawyers envy. Steve Fretzin is a lawyer coach who specializing in helping attorneys to build the practices they want. Find some of his top tips in his new book, aptly-titled Be That Lawyer!"
Jared Correia, Red Cave Law Firm Consulting

"Steve Fretzin combines his profound knowledge about the practice of law with his boundless imagination for meaningful strategies and tactics to attract ever better work. What I like best about Steve's work is that he sets our minds going in the right direction and we can individually build on that momentum in our individual creative ways."
Gerry Riskin, Founder of Edge International

"Steve Fretzin has created numerous terrific business development resources, networks, and tactics that are designed to raise lawyer profiles, and to better foster client relationships. As a brand and PR specialist for lawyers, I appreciate Steve's understanding of the importance of integrating tactics for a more efficient and effective sales process and program. He's a lot of fun to talk with too!"
Terry M. Isner, Owner/CEO of Jaffe

Other books by Steve Fretzin:

➢ Sales-Free Selling: The Death of Sales and the Rise of a New Methodology

➢ The Attorney's Networking Handbook: 14 Principles to Growing Your Law Practice in Less Time and with Greater Results

➢ The Ambitious Attorney: Your Guide to Doubling or Even Tripling Your Book of Business

All three books are available on Amazon.

- Are you conducting presentations and getting little value from your time invested? No worries, it's also here.
- Is your mindset positive about business development and growing your book of business? Oh yeah, we have the goods.
- Does the concept of cross-marketing have you stumped? Come on, you know it's here!
- Is your infomercial stale and therefore totally unmemorable? You guessed it. You'll read it here.

ile this book may not handle every single possible nario you may run across, I do have my finger on pulse of the legal industry and what lawyers are llenged by every day. Take what you can from what learned and perfected on legal business elopment, marketing and networking to make it r own. My greatest hope is to hear from you neday that you did take action and that this book de the difference for you in your legal career. So oy the book, take lots of notes and most portantly, BE THAT LAWYER!

~ Steve Fretzin

Legal Business Development Isn't Rocket Science

250+ Easy & Actionable Ways to Grow Your Book of Business (In Less Time and with Greater Results)

Steve Fretzin

INTRODUCTION

If you're reading this book, it's clear th
about your future as a lawyer. You und
developing your own clients permits yo
your career trajectory and overall desti
question you need to ask yourself is, *Ar
apply and execute on what I'm reading*
think about the answer in your head, an
"yes" or a "no?" This book, my other thr
all the content I've ever produced is wor
take no action to apply it. That's just me
with you up front.

I wish I could tell you that there were so
technical components to legal business o
that can only be explained by me. That's
the case. The title of the book clearly stat
NOT teaching rocket science, but that sta
doesn't make it easy to digest or execute
you might get angry that business develo
taught in law school or by the leadership

The good news is that all of the content fr
books, videos, articles and even my podca
tactical and actionable steps and languag
learn and execute to get real results. This
so many things, with over 250 plus takeav
paying attention. It will answer questions

Does your networking group seem like a v
time? The solution you need is in here.

FORWARD

Business development and client service are twin passions of mine. In my 40 years of lawyering, there are few I have encountered who understand business development and client service intuitively. Steve Fretzin is one of those rare persons.

Steve's passion is helping lawyers navigate the unique challenges and opportunities of developing and executing successful marketing strategies and brand building in the legal field. He understands how to help, teach, and create success for lawyers who aspire to be at the top of their game. The invaluable lessons and perspectives I have learned from Steve over the last decade are herein his latest book. It is a "must-read" for any lawyer who seeks to improve their marketing and business development and get to the next level of success in their careers.

Throughout my four decades in legal practice, the role of personal brand marketing has made an enormous contribution to my own business development efforts. By utilizing many of the key business development strategies found in Steve's book, lawyers can implement a tested approach to engaging clients and providing them with solutions and tailored business development methodologies.

Steve has established himself as the go-to person in this space. This book should be at the top of the syllabus for every marketing course available in our profession.

~ Jerry Maatman

Jerry Maatman is a partner in the Chicago and New York offices of Seyfarth Shaw LLP. He co-chairs the firm's class action defense group. Jerry is an acknowledged thought leader on client service and business development. His focus and passion for driving new business enabled him to become a top originator at his firm. He is also an adjunct professor at Northwestern University School of Law, where he has taught trial advocacy for 30 years.

ACKNOWLEDGMENTS

First off, I'd like to thank all of my successful clients, strategic partners, and friends who inspire me every day to continue working and playing in the legal space. My goal every day is to help attorneys to grow successful law practices. Second, my amazing editors Emma Zelewsky an Sue Robinson. Lastly, I must acknowledge my incredibly supportive and loving wife Lisa, who continues to support my goals and dreams as an entrepreneur.

TABLE OF CONTENTS

Part 1: Business Development

TABLE OF CONTENTS

Part 2: Marketing

Part 3: Networking

TABLE OF CONTENTS

TABLE OF CONTENTS

Part 4: Practice Management

PART 1:
BUSINESS DEVELOPMENT

CHAPTER 1

GOING FOR NEW BUSINESS? DON'T LET THINGS HAPPEN, HAVE A PLAN

Imagine it's Thanksgiving dinner and the whole family is sitting around the table waiting for the feast to begin. Unfortunately, something is different this year.

The table isn't set. It's barren, just a big empty wooden table. Now, as if things weren't strange enough, mom comes out with the most beautiful bird you've ever seen — just dumps it in the middle of the table! Then, she rapidly empties out the dressing, cranberries and sweet potatoes all on top, in one heaping mess. Everyone is truly mortified. Has mom lost her mind?

Now, let's come back to reality and discuss what this scenario has to do with business development and having an agenda. Well, if you are walking into pitch meetings without setting an agenda with your prospective client, you should think again about my Thanksgiving dinner scenario. It's very possible that you might be sitting at that messy table and not even realizing it.

One of the most important elements to walking a buyer through a buying decision is maintaining control of the meeting. While it might feel natural to pitch, solve and provide your rate structures, most rainmakers know that free consulting isn't the best approach to business development anymore.

The mantra that I teach my clients is, "Prescription before diagnosis is malpractice." Therefore, it is mission critical to ask, listen and learn before providing your fancy pitch. This is why establishing a win-win agenda for you and your prospect is so important.

Below, I've highlighted the actual scripting for you to use. It's incredibly powerful, just ask any of my clients who now close deals with ease.

Step 1: Make it permission based.
After taking some time building rapport with a new prospective client, you could say, "Listen, Terry, I know how valuable your time is, and mine as well. I thought in order to make the best use of our time together today, it would be OK for me to establish an agenda. Is that good with you?"

The important element here is to get buy-in from your prospect. The language is very important because it establishes the key point of "making the best use of our time." This is something everyone is looking for.

Step 2: Establish the time and make it uninterrupted.
While it might be fine for a good meeting to go on far longer than anticipated, what about the meetings that are not going anywhere?

The last thing you can afford to do is invest two hours with someone who is totally unqualified to work with you or has no interest. Therefore, setting the stage for a 45- to 60-

minute meeting might be the better play. You can always let it go longer if things are looking up.

Also, you may want to subtly ask for "uninterrupted time" to ensure that your meeting doesn't get hijacked by a lousy cellphone call. These disruptions can totally sideline a good meeting. In this situation, you might say, "I know we had discussed keeping the meeting to an hour, Terry, is that still OK for you? Great, and I'm going to shut my phone off so we won't be interrupted." This is an easy way to set the tone for your prospect to put her phone away.

Step 3: Define the purpose.
While there are hundreds of options for this step, I'm only going to suggest one. Make the purpose of the meeting intentionally vague.

You would say, "As I see it, the purpose of the meeting today is to learn more about one another and see if there's a fit to work together."

The goal of this point is to show the prospect that only a "fit for both parties" makes an engagement work. It also sets you up on the same level playing field with Mrs. Big Shot CEO or general counsel. From my experience, getting into the weeds with your prospect on the various elements of the case in the early stages of a meeting like this is a huge mistake.

Step 4: Defining expectations for both parties.
If you recall, I mentioned the importance of asking first and solving later. In this step, we establish the order of events about to unfold. You would say, "To see if there's a fit, I'd like to start out our meeting today by asking you more

questions about your situation (or whatever the problem may be). I also tend to ask tough questions, is that OK with you?"

So, you might get the "asking questions" part of my script, but why did I mention "tough questions?" The goal of the meeting is not just to learn about someone's problems, but rather, how urgent they are to solve. This urgency can be developed not by convincing, but by asking those tougher questions and finding the prospect's pain.

By gaining permission to ask the tougher questions, it may force you to actually ask deeper questions than you usually do. I also ask, "What are your expectations for today's meeting, Terry?" as a way to keep her engaged and to make this agenda more collaborative.

Step 5: Define a win-win outcome.
Before getting into this step, I'd like to do a little setup with you. What's the worst outcome from a new prospect meeting? Is it when they say no? In today's politically correct world, buyers hate saying no. Mainly because they are afraid that you might not take no for an answer and keep selling.

They've been oversold before and detested the feeling, just like you do. So, what's the typical response when you want to tell someone no, but don't want to deal with them any further? Yes, it's the old "I want to think about it" routine. If you hear this from a prospect, know that you are most likely not getting this business.

Now, that being said, we need to get to the truth with every prospect we can. Therefore, the best outcome for the

meeting is getting to a "Yes, let's move forward on this matter."

Or get them to say "no," so you can both move on. For the record, I relish every "no" that I hear from attorneys. If it's not a fit, why would we want to work together, anyway?

As far as the script for this agenda, you would say, "At the end of our meeting, I'd like to suggest one or two possible directions. If we agree there's a fit and we want to move forward together, that would be great. Also, if we find that there isn't a fit for whatever reason, I'd like us to agree up front to call it a no and walk away friends. Does that sound fair to you?"

Now, if you're like most attorneys, you're saying to yourself, "I can't see myself saying or asking that to a CEO or GC."

I would respond and say, "That's too bad." Because getting to the truth and having a prospect be honest with you is critical to saving you time and getting to a result quickly.

This outcome also releases any sales stress that might accompany the meeting. Giving permission for your prospect to say no will help her to relax and trust you in the process. In the end, the ability to get buy-in and take control of the prospect meeting is critical to success.

Without process, you're winging it. I rarely hear success stories from someone winging it. I hope you can practice and try this agenda out for yourself. It is truly remarkable the difference it can make in your meetings.

CHAPTER 2

DEVELOPING BUSINESS TAKES THE SAME PREPARATION NEEDED TO GO TO COURT

One of the easiest ways to explain how to be a successful business developer is by using the analogy of a lawyer conducting a murder trial.

While this might be a strange way to illustrate my philosophy on business development, I ask you to bear with me as I promise to produce a solid "ah-ha" moment for you before the completion of my chapter.

Imagine you are engaged in the murder trial of the century. The suspect is being held without bail and you are diligently developing the best case. In reviewing all of the facts, evidence and proof, you disappointingly realize that all you have is one witness.

This individual claims to have witnessed the homicide from only a few hundred feet away. Unfortunately, the witness is severely nearsighted, has a criminal record and is a notorious snitch. As the prosecutor, how are you feeling about your case? How will this case hold up in court?

While this may seem like a ridiculous scenario, when we relate it back to business development, it can take a more serious tone.

To grow one's law practice, attorneys today must successfully identify evidence that a prospective client has needs, issues and compelling reasons to proceed with any matter. As you know, CEOs and general counsels don't typically leave their existing counsel without significant cause.

Your ability to identify the key factors of pain, fear or gain may be the difference between new business and wasting your valuable time. Here are three key areas that will definitely make you a better business developer and maybe even a better friend, lawyer or spouse.

1. Build rapport first.

It's important for the jury to like you when you're trying to win them over to your side. The same is true when meeting with a new prospective client. Be sure to invest some time at the beginning of your meeting to ask some well-prepared questions and get her talking about her favorite subject — herself.

For example, you might ask, "I noticed your business was rated by INC. magazine as a top place to work last year. How did you build such a strong work environment?" Or, "I saw on LinkedIn that you run marathons for the American Cancer Society charity. When did you begin running for charity?" Being prepared and getting your prospects talking about their favorite subjects is critical to developing rapport and trust.

2. Qualify all prospective clients on the phone before meeting them in person.

Try to be patient and not scramble to meet with anyone who's breathing. Take a few minutes on the phone to ask some qualifying questions. After developing some rapport on the phone just say, "To make the best use of our time when we do meet, may I ask you a few questions to better understand the situation?"

Then dive in with some solid qualifying questions to better understand if there really is a matter here or not. Asking a few good questions on the phone will save you time, money and the frustration of meeting with unqualified prospects. Be sure to ask the following questions on the phone before meeting:

• "Tell me what's been going on?"
• "What are your primary challenges, frustrations and concerns about (their needs)?"

Be sure to obtain one to three issues on the phone. This will give you enough "evidence" to commit your time to meet. Also, do not discuss legal solutions on the phone! Get the prospect talking and feeling good about you and your ability to listen. Then schedule the in-person meeting to discuss solutions after you've given it some thought (even when she meets with you, ask more questions before solving or offering advice).

A good way to deflect her advances on solutions is to say, "Prescription before diagnosis is malpractice." Giving away advice can eliminate the reason for meeting, which is where the magic happens.

3. Prepare your evidence in advance.

When a prospective client tells you her issues, you should think of this as "collecting evidence" or reasons to work together. The more in-depth questions you ask, the more evidence there is for you to engage in a new matter.

The best advice I can give to any attorney is to ask deeper questions to better understand the pain points of your prospective new client. Your ability to uncover these pain points will directly impact her decision to work with you. Here are some questions that will help you to draw out proof that this decision-maker needs to hire you:

• "With regards to your legal needs, what are your greatest challenges, frustrations and concerns?" (Ask if you haven't already.)

• "What have you done to address this issue prior to meeting with me today?"

• "How much is this problem costing you?"

• "How has this problem impacted the company and you on a personal level?"

• "What happens if nothing is done to solve these issues?"

• "On a scale of one to 10, how serious are these issues we're discussing today?"

• "Who have you used in the past and why are you thinking of changing counsel?"

• "Other than yourself, who else might be involved in making this decision?"

Think of the power you will hold when someone shares her deepest fears and pains with you. This approach will not only make you a trusted partner, but it eliminates the need to storm in and pitch right away.

Most lawyers find it's easiest to sell by talking about what they know best, the law. There is a term for this, and it's called "free consulting." The best rainmakers today are the ones who ask questions, listen and empathize.

The same skills you use in the courtroom need to be applied in the way you conduct your business development meetings with prospective new clients.

By building more rapport, qualifying on the phone and taking a deeper dive when meeting, you will find greater success when doing business development.

CHAPTER 3

BEING YOUR OWN RAINMAKER IS THE BEST WAY TO SUCCEED

It's happening every day. Change. Just read the Daily Law Bulletin or National Law Review. New law firm mergers and buyouts are becoming commonplace. Law firms are looking more like a business and less like the Wild West. It's a reality that the firm you work at today, may not be the same firm tomorrow.

While that could be a blessing or a curse, the common theme on the street for every attorney still remains, "What's your book of business?" Why is that so important today versus in the past? Let's take a closer look at the facts so that you can make an important life decision this year.

Fact No. 1: According to a Law.com article, law firm mergers are happening at a record pace. Currently, there are approximately six to eight mergers per month happening nationally.

Whether you are on the buy side or the sell side of a merger, it may not matter. Many of these mergers create an opportunity to trim the fat.

It should not be a surprise that attorneys with a sustainable book of business are not considered "fat." Doing good work for your rainmaking partner just isn't enough anymore. Without having your own clients and driving business to the firm, you may be setting yourself up for disaster.

Fact No. 2: Being a business development coach for lawyers, I find myself interacting with legal recruiters from time to time. They regularly indicate that staff attorneys aren't as marketable and get paid significantly less as an inbound lateral.

In speaking with Chris White of The Gunther Group, he said, "In our recent experience, compensation for partners with a book of business valued between $500K and $1 million at midmarket firms can expect compensation ranging from $250K to $500K.

Without business, compensation could fall 20 percent to 30 percent, and would likely be significantly less (40 percent-plus) compared to partners nearing $1 million in originations. Importantly, midmarket firms rarely seek partners without a book of business except when they have a pressing need."

What does this mean for you? While some opportunities arise from time to time for an in-house role or at another firm, the only real job security needs to be created by you. If you read my monthly column, you know there are many skills that need to be learned (and they are learned, not innate) to make business development easier and even enjoyable.

It's critical that you find internal and external resources to gain these skills. We are only one recession away from another 2008 when lawyers were being released and displaced at record numbers.

Fact No. 3: The American Bar Association released its Legal Professional Statistics in November regarding the lawyer population and it's never been higher. There are currently 1,338,678 attorneys nationally and 63,422 in the state of Illinois alone.

With competition at a record high, it's never been more important to separate yourself from the crowd. Marketing yourself and your unique set of skills is the answer for many successful attorneys.

Ask yourself, "Who's the most successful attorney in my practice area?" Then work diligently to get there in the next two, five or 10 years. Working on your business development skills and personal branding today will be critical to your future. The good news is that most attorneys aren't doing this yet, so by starting now, you can work to get ahead of the curve.

Fact No. 4: The baby boomers are slowly retiring and it's not going the way we all thought. In the past, it was assumed that an elder's book of business would trickle down to the service partners' book in the form of originations. In today's business environment, it's not financially beneficial or even feasible for the firm to give full originations credit when the rainmaker steps down.

Hiding behind the older rainmakers and waiting for them to retire or die just isn't a foolproof plan anymore (and it's a little morbid, too).

While it's possible that you are due some reward for all of your hard-earned hours with his or her clients, counting on that may be the kiss of death for you. Balance your time on billing and originating to ensure you're setting yourself up for success in the future.

As I mentioned above, utilize all of the resources available to you. Work daily to learn, execute and grow your own practice. If you happen to get some credit on a matter you've worked on in the past, it's just icing on the cake.

At the end of the day, it's really "You Inc." and must be treated as such. Developing your book and having your own clients is not an option anymore if you're looking for independence, security and financial freedom. Creating new originations may seem like a second job, but with focused learning and execution you can still have the balance you need to be happy.

CHAPTER 4

BUSINESS DEVELOPMENT LESSONS FROM THE PUTTING GREEN TO THE LAW FIRM

Over the past 30 years, I have played hundreds of rounds of golf, never thinking much about how it related to business development. I was too busy swinging away, just trying to get to the next tee box without losing my ball.

A few years ago I met a golf instructor and decided to take a few lessons. It was a good thing I did because it not only improved my game, it provided a supplementary experience that really struck a chord with me as it related to business development.

As an attorney, you've probably been involved in a "pitch" meeting with a prospective client. You may recall the nervousness or anxiousness felt around the idea of signing up a piece of new business.

During your meeting, you probably believe that the end result or "close" is the single most important element of the meeting. While your origination numbers may depend on closing the deal, there is another important aspect to running a successful business development meeting that holds the key to your success.

Let me go back to my golf pro and explain. After meeting and chatting with my new golf pro for a few minutes, he invited me on to the green carpet to take a few swings. He watched me intently for a few minutes as I stepped up and smashed a few balls into the range.

Finally, he turned to me and said, "Steve, do you enjoy swinging the golf club?"

Being terribly confused by his question I said, "What?" I simply had no idea what he was talking about. Fortunately, he explained, "You seem to be approaching each swing with the intention of getting to the outcome as fast as possible. You don't seem to be enjoying the actual swing."

I paused and thought about that for a minute. Do I really enjoy swinging a golf club or am I just trying to get it over with, hoping to land the ball somewhere inbounds? I then realized there was very little enjoyment in swinging the golf club, and I was in fact rushing each shot to quickly get to an outcome.

For me, this conversation was a real epiphany. If the sport of golf is all about swinging a golf club repeatedly, and I'm not enjoying the swing, then am I really enjoying the game of golf? Pretty deep, right?

At the time, I didn't have the skill sets to truly enjoy the swing. Therefore, I was only focused on the end result of each shot. The true enjoyment of golf is in the beauty and enjoyment of each swing. It then became clear to me that a better, more fluid swing will produce a much better outcome.

This is where the missing piece of the puzzle was for me. It's also where I realized how perfectly this scenario relates to attorneys and the process of business development.

As I thought more about the swing in golf and what happens in a typical pitch meeting, there was something unnatural about both of these activities. Just like my wild and harried swing, rushing to pitch a prospective client can lead to an unpredictable outcome.

A better approach would be to slow things down and enjoy conducting a successful business meeting. Instead of rushing to pitch and talk about yourself, you would build rapport and focus on asking great questions.

While this might go against one's natural instincts to problem solve, it will be a refreshing change to focus on not solving problems. By concentrating on asking tough questions and uncovering a prospective client's pain points, there will be more urgency for them to hire you.

The enjoyment of the swing in business development is to be found in the relationship building and questioning process that allows us to truly understand our prospective client's problems, needs and desires.

If you focus your time and attention there, they have to believe that you are indeed an expert and someone with whom they should be working. Having your focus on the prospective client and not on yourself can only help you in developing a new client opportunity. It might also separate you from the other attorneys who are still hacking away with their salesy pitches.

As you think about this new process of walking a buyer through a buying decision, you can truly enjoy your business development efforts and take away the pressure to simply close the sale. When the process is all about the buyer, good results will just happen.

CHAPTER 5

TAKING SELLING OUT OF CLIENT PROSPECTING

As a lawyer, you probably despise the word "sales." This word has justly taken its share of lumps over the past 100 years as soapbox salesmen and carpetbaggers made profits off of uneducated patsies.

I'm sure the thought of pushing legal services on the people you know isn't an appealing proposition to you. Sound about right?

When comparing the differences between sales and business development, you must first look at the definition of "sales." "Selling" is defined as the act of providing a product or service in exchange for money.

For some reason this implies that you are attempting to convince someone to buy what you are selling. The traditional "pitch meeting" model was created to convince and motivate a buyer into making a buying decision.

This happens soon after meeting a new prospective client as you attempt to demonstrate your verbal and legal prowess. The majority of sales professionals and yes, even attorneys follow a similar path with their buyers.

In teaching business development for more than 15 years, I have found that the model for "selling" must change to include little actual pitching or selling. The key difference in the traditional model of sales and what I call, "sales-free selling," is that we must not present solutions and rates until we clearly understand the prospective client's issues, needs and compelling reasons to act. This is not an easy thing to accomplish, which is why most attorneys fall back on simply making the pitch.

In today's competitive market, making pitches too early can lead to providing free advice without ever obtaining the new client. I use the medical analogy, "prescription before diagnosis is malpractice," to help emphasize the importance of holding back on your pitch until you better understand the prospect's needs and motivation for changing her existing situation.

The skills involved in questioning, listening and empathizing are incredibly difficult to master. Here are some tips that might help you get on the right track.

Tip No. 1: Build rapport.
It's very hard to get information from someone who doesn't like to trust you. In the first five or 10 minutes of a business meeting, focus on your prospective client. If you did your pre-meeting research, use that information to ask questions and get him or her talking. Try to find commonalities that will bond you before moving on to business.

Tip No. 2: The most important question in any business meeting is ...

An effective approach to a business meeting is to invest more time questioning the buyer. Be prepared to ask 15 to 40 minutes of questions to ensure that every issue, need or pain point is uncovered.

Start slow with some basic background questions to better understand their business dynamics. Then, lead into asking, "What are your challenges, frustrations or concerns related to the legal side of your business?"

This question can be altered as you see fit, but the point is to ask about their issues to better understand how you might be able to help solve them.

Tip No. 3: If you find a nugget of gold, keep digging.
Once you have a few issues on the table, keep digging to find what the prospect's frustrations, costs and impacts are as it relates to these issues. One trick is to ask your prospective client to provide specific examples of their issues.

When telling stories, people tend to provide more details and get more emotional. This will build a higher level of understanding to determine if the prospective client is even a "fit" to work with you.

Asking great questions proves that you are an expert without ever saying so. Your goal should be to expose the prospects compelling reasons to change that drives urgency. As you might already know, asking questions is the single best way to comprehend someone's needs.

When I think about salespeople's methods in a traditional sense, I can feel my skin crawl a little. My wife will tell you that I despise being sold to more than anyone.

The beauty of learning business development is that you won't have to "sell" anyone anything.

My clients focus on building rapport, asking amazing questions and qualifying whom to invest more time with or whom to kick to the curb before too much time is wasted!

The reality is that knowing more about your prospects saves you time from selling and chasing the ones that were never going to hire you anyway.

The best part about a sales-free selling process is how you will make the buyer feel. Not only will he or she like and trust you, they will feel confident that you are the right person to help with his or her legal needs.

So, forget being "salesy" and focus on walking a buyer through a buying decision. There's no better or noble thing one can do than to solve problems for others.

CHAPTER 6

NO GENDER BARRIER FOR BUSINESS DEVELOPMENT

In knowing, working with and interviewing hundreds of women in law, I've observed a fair amount of angst regarding business development and growing a book of business.

I have heard comments ranging from, "It's still a man's world" or "As a woman, it's hard to be direct when asking for business." Whatever the case, the reality is that there's never been a better time in history to be a female attorney than right now.

The New York Times published a piece back in 2016 that showed women overtaking men in law school for the first time ever. Look around you, women are in lead general counsel roles, growing their own law firms and hustling internally to become the rainmakers of the future.

If you're looking for recognition, opportunity and freedom from the shackles of a 60-hour workweek, be sure to make learning business development a significant part of your lawyer lifestyle. To make this transformation of worker bee to business development assassin, here are three easy to implement tips that work for women in growing a book and taking your career to the next level.

Tip 1: Become an expert at time management

With the billable hour, family emergencies and personal obligations all weighing you down, it is critical to get organized right now. The easiest way to do this is to buy the book titled "Getting Things Done" by David Allen. I am a huge fan.

In addition to turning my life around, I have pushed his concepts to my busiest lawyer clients who immediately see results from his concepts. Without getting extra organized with your time, you may be doomed to fail as a developer of new business. Remember, if you won't take the time to read a book on time management, how are you ever going to truly manage your time?

Tip 2: Learn or do something with business development every day.

If you truly want to get ahead in growing your law practice, you need to become a student of business development. An easy way to do this is to commit to learning or doing one thing every day to advance your interests.

A few suggestions might include reading a chapter of a business development book, watching a video or attending a business development or marketing course focused on CLE. You may also want to e-mail one contact, client or friend for a coffee in order to open new doors that may seem shut.

One of the best tools for this is LinkedIn. There isn't a reason why you couldn't look through one of your connections on LinkedIn each day to see what GC, CEO or HR director he or she might be connected to. By making business development and learning a part of your daily routine, you create an "inner-culture" for yourself that will elevate your game.

Tip No. 3: It's not about being a man or a woman, it's about being the best!
One of the greatest tips I can share with you is that there are advantages to being a man and advantages in being a woman in law. What you need to do is rise above that and become excellent!

Now, there are two types of excellent. First, you must become an amazing and dynamic attorney that people are impressed with. This one point alone can make your career. Second, you must have an approach to business development that will separate you from the pack.

While everyone else is in fear to ask his or her contacts for quality introductions into the midmarket, for example, you could have an approach that is effective to get you in the door and closing that new corporate client.

When everyone else is busy pitching, convincing and flaunting his or her legal prowess to prospective buyers, you could be busy asking, listening and understanding their needs and pains.

As a coach and trainer exclusively for attorneys, I am in the unique position to see and hear things that you may not. Many of the women that I work with start out with the same concerns you might have about balancing family, work and relationships. In the end, you have to decide what's most important to you and where you want to devote time. If you can slowly work business development into that mix, you may see advancement on the horizon.

CHAPTER 7

UNCERTAIN TIMES ARE ALWAYS A GOOD TIME TO CHECK FUTURE BUSINESS OPPORTUNITIES

Every time you speak with a client, there are opportunities that can be uncovered to help her, while also identifying additional work.

Your ability to execute and run an effective meeting with your client can mean the difference between having yet another year, or realizing an incredible breakthrough year!

It doesn't take much time to accomplish. You only need to have the skills to set up the meeting, ask questions and follow up to gain the traction you're looking for.

When meeting with an existing or past client, it's mission-critical that you actively ask and listen to get more detailed information than you may have in the past. Here's what you probably accomplished in the past when meeting a client for lunch:

- Socialized and built rapport.
- Discussed current and past matters.
- Enjoyed a delicious lunch.

While those are great starting points, what about:

• Asking questions to uncover new and interesting legal issues?

• Uncovering opportunities to cross-market?

• Identifying quality introductions that could be made for you?

• Creating opportunities to be a resource for your client?

As you can see, the difference in these two scenarios is quite different as it relates to building long-lasting relationships, obtaining more work and truly helping your client to solve problems. Here are three suggestions that I work on with my attorney clients to make their meetings more focused and beneficial.

Tip No. 1

Consider setting an agenda on the phone prior to meeting your client. The idea here is that you can set yourself up to have a more impactful meeting before it has even begun. The key is to set the table with a game plan to help your client better prepare for the meeting.

One way to lay the groundwork is to ask, "So Barbara, before we meet for lunch next week, I wanted to set some expectations and goals for our meeting, is that OK?" She will be very agreeable to this. Then say, "Terrific. In addition to reviewing our current IP work together, I'd like to discuss your business as a whole to better understand the big picture for your growth. I know these are crazy times and a number of my clients are concerned with the state of things. Would that be alright with you?"

The point here is that you are setting the table for a more detailed conversation about her business to see the big picture and identify "gaps" in their legal or business strategy. This may lead to additional work for you, your firm's partners or your referral sources that you need to keep fed.

Tip No. 2

The next step is to come to the meeting with some great questions that may lead to additional work or cross-marketing opportunities. Try to keep the questions open ended and work with her responses to take a deeper dive if possible.

Here are a few sample questions and the possible follow-up questions that will allow you to dig deeper. In this example, I'll continue to be an IP attorney at a full-service firm.

• With all of the craziness going on politically, what are some of your greatest concerns as it relates to your business?

• Tell me more about that?

• Tell me more about the other legal work that you deal with that isn't focused on IP?

• How are they taking care of you and your sensitivity to excessive billing?

• Where are the key growth areas for the company this year?

• How can I help you to achieve those goals?

• In doing IP work with many international companies, many of my clients ask me employment and immigration questions. Tell me about the recent and future issues you see occurring in these areas?

• I know you've mentioned to me on several occasions how pleased you've been with my work the past few years. Who else should I be speaking with that might be able to utilize my experience?

• Would you be open to talking with him about the successes we've had together and see if he'll be open to speaking with me?

• Other than legal specific work, how can I be of value to you or your company?

• What other business issues are you having?

As you can see from these examples, there are so many paths that you can go down to find new opportunities.If your client is open to these questions, you may uncover that she is dissatisfied with her other lawyers or that there's a blind spot in their business that may put her at risk. Asking questions shows a level of caring on your part because you want to learn more about her business and assist wherever possible. It's a win-win if ever there was one.

Tip No. 3

Ok, you've set the table and asked the questions. Now you have to follow up and discuss next steps. If there's a legal issue, set up a follow-up call to review. If there's an introduction that's been offered, agree on a next step to ensure that it's followed through on. When dealing with an extremely busy client who has offered up a quality introduction, you may want to ask, "I know how busy you get, Barbara. If I don't hear from you regarding your friend Bob, how would you like me to follow up with you?"

This question is terrific for moving the introduction forward and having a unobtrusive way of checking in without bothering your client too much.

When thinking about your clients, it's imperative that you put them first. I'm sure we can all agree on that. Focus on asking great questions, listening and following through to provide the best experience for the client, while also uncovering opportunities for additional work and introductions.

These are challenging and unsure times for all of us. Our clients need us more than ever, so make the most of each engagement and you'll see greater results for your client and in building your book of business.

CHAPTER 8

THREE TIPS FOR YOUNG LAWYERS ON HOW TO BRING IN THE BUSINESS

As a young lawyer, there are a number of confusing and conflicting theories about business development and what role it should play in your life.

You may hear things from your firm's leadership, marketing department or colleagues that sound like:

• "Business development is nothing to concern yourself with yet."

• "You're too new to worry about learning business development. Just focus on learning the law."

• "Just wait until you make income partner, then you'll make time for it."

• "If you're not making money from your business development efforts, why bother?"

While there may be smatterings of truth in each of these statements, it's important for you to do your own research and make up your own mind about business development.

Making good choices is all about looking at the benefits for the time invested and deciding if you're willing to commit to the effort. If your eyes are open, it will be easier to see the path clearly ahead of you. To assist with this, here are three thought-provoking tips to help you understand if business development is right for you and how to get started.

Young Lawyer Tip No. 1: Be a great lawyer first

Yes, it's true. To be a great business developer, you must first be a great lawyer. Learning your craft is the single most important factor to shaping your future as a successful attorney. No matter what area of the law you are practicing, it's important to think about your future now and what type of law you want to practice. Here are three key elements to consider as you sharpen your legal skills:

1. Try to focus on the area of law that is most interesting to you. If you enjoy real estate, invest your time in that area. If you like to debate, focus on litigation. If there's something that you are passionate about, don't wait to get involved. While this might seem obvious, there are thousands of attorneys practicing in areas that are not interesting to them. When work is interesting or even fun, it can take away a lot of the day-to-day pressures that many lawyers face.

2. Find a great mentor with whom you can learn. Even if your direct boss doesn't have time for you, make an effort to find a strong mentor elsewhere. This can mean the difference between success and failure as an attorney and as a business developer. Having someone to talk to who has "been there and done that" will help you keep your perspective.

Be sure to meet regularly and ask lots of questions. Most successful attorneys use mentors and coaches to help them to make positive changes throughout a career. These internal or external relationships also play a role if you decide to change practice areas or firms in the future.

3. Be a sponge! I've heard the saying, "If I'm not learning, I'm dying." So, whether you read the American Bar Association newsletter regularly, attend regular Continuing Legal Education events or listen to podcasts of attorneys speaking about the law, it's important to keep learning.

Some of my clients have built their reputations and books on staying current with the ever-changing legal system and laws in their areas of practice. Look into the future if you can and try to see what's coming up the pike that you can learn about and speak on before anyone else.

Young Lawyer Tip No. 2: Don't Sell... Network!

For most young attorneys, your job shouldn't be trying to close million-dollar deals with 60-year-old CEOs. It's just not realistic to do so. Rather, start planning and executing on a networking strategy to develop contacts that will lead to long-term business opportunities. Here are three ideas to follow in order to accomplish this task:

1. Failure to plan is a plan to fail. While you might have the best intentions, it's hard to get out there and network with all of the hours you are putting in at the office. Create a simple plan that allows you to focus your time in the right places with the right people.

Think about your friends, family, past co-workers and business professionals that you already know. Take the time to make a list and rank them based on "relationship" and "potential to help you." You may realize that you've got some terrific people to meet with and keep close to.

It's also helpful to set activity goals for yourself. You might want to take two breakfast meetings a week with these friends or attend one networking event a month. Try to use this plan to keep your activity levels up, even when the work is pouring in. There's always time to eat an early meal, bring in lunch or have a drink after hours. Scheduling the time is always better than hoping it happens.

2. Learn how to be an effective networker. In my experience, networking can be a huge drain of time and resources if not done with "intent." This means that you should study the art of networking and understand the best ways to proceed, rather than going out there winging it.

By selecting groups and events that are synergistic with your goals, you will have a much better overall experience. Do your research online or talk to your mentors before heading out to attend various events.

For example, if you're an intellectual property attorney, try to find a networking group with attorneys in other practice areas. This way you can all refer one another without conflicts. Or if you are focused on helping small business, try to attend events where the business owners participate. Try to find out in advance how many other attorneys typically attend to ensure you're not one of 20 in the room.

3. To get ramped up more quickly, try to network with the people you know best. Call up your high school, undergrad and law school friends to meet for coffee or drinks. When you meet, use that time to ask about his or her personal life, job and overall business. Learn what his or her needs are and see if there's a way to help.

If she's looking for a new condominium, make an introduction to a successful real estate person you know. Or help her find a new job if she's unhappy at work. In addition to making you feel great, you are setting the foundation for a cooperative business relationship in the future. Be sure to stay in close contact with the friends who may be able to use you or refer you.

Young Lawyer Tip No. 3: You're a millennial, use social media to stay connected.
While Facebook and Twitter are great for staying in touch and conveying messages, try focusing on LinkedIn for growing your law practice. Most business professionals are on it, but not using it for specific purposes. There are three key elements to being successful in leveraging this technology to your advantage.

First, you must develop a solid profile. People are watching you and you may not even realize it. Having a profile that is incomplete or inaccurate can hurt your image. It's similar to a resume that is riddled with typos. Invest 20 minutes and look at some creative and more elaborate LinkedIn profiles of your peers. Mimic what they are doing and update your profile until you reach 100 percent complete.

Second, develop an appropriate strategy for what you are trying to accomplish. If you aren't looking to meet or talk with anyone, don't set up a profile and stay off the site. If you are looking to get out there and promote your expertise, connect with the people who can help you advance your interests.

If you're like me and want the world to see you, be more open to allowing a variety of new people to connect with you. That being said, I don't want to connect with total strangers. Unless they write and tell me why connecting would be of value, I will usually not accept their request to connect.

The third and most important element of using LinkedIn is to use it to leverage your best connections to get quality introductions. The greatest benefit of this platform is being able to actually see whom your connections know.

For example, let's say I have a client who became a friend. I can go into his profile and pull up all of his connections. If there is one that seems like the perfect introduction for me, I could simply ask him what he thinks. Based on his response, I would follow up and ask him to make a call on my behalf to his friend and introduce me.

It's just that simple. I have been teaching LinkedIn for years, and it's been a proven winner for new lead generation for attorneys.

There needs to be balance in developing a strong practice as a young professional. Your direct income, job security and freedom may all be at risk without it.

While the emphasis should be on learning the law, and gaining valuable experience, you need to think strategically about your future as well. Start planning for business development now and you may surpass many of your peers in the near future.

It's not a sprint to the finish line, but rather a marathon. As long as you stay the course and work intelligently over time, good things will happen for you and your practice.

CHAPTER 9

HOW TO BE A BETTER PUBLIC SPEAKER — AND GENERATE MORE BUSINESS

Over the past 15 years, I have spoken about business development to help professionals obtain more business from their efforts. These groups have ranged from five people to more than 1,000. At the end of the day, there are two purposes to speaking that are paramount.

First, it's about building your name and brand to be seen as an expert in your chosen field. Second, it's to get actual business from the time invested. The unfortunate truth for many attorneys is that they may not be accomplishing either one of these goals.

Here are three tips that I help my clients with on a regular basis. In some cases, these tips have been game changers in their careers.

Tip No. 1: Choose wisely when deciding where to speak
One of the biggest mistakes I'm witnessing is attorneys who will speak practically anywhere to try to get their names out there and attract new business. While this might be OK to try out new material or build your speaking skills, finding the right place and audience is really where the value is.

When thinking about your target audience, I always recommend two categories: First, the people who actually buy legal services like CEOs, CFOs and general counsel; second, the people who can routinely refer you to the people who buy legal services like attorneys in other practice areas, accountants, bankers and so forth.

While it's not always easy to get audiences like these, it's what you need to shoot for to build your book as a speaker in your marketplace.

One example of a failure to identify the right audience occurred with one of my clients about a year ago. He is a well-regarded speaker in the mergers and acquisition field. He's always out there speaking and sharing his words of wisdom. The problem we found was in his audience — other M&A attorneys.

Essentially, he was sharing his work, ideas and research with his competition, with the hope that someone would refer him. When I asked how many referrals he had received over the past 10 years of speaking to his peers, the look in his face said it all. Zero point zero.

Now, I'm sure there are exceptions where magic happened and big deals were landed with the wrong audience, but we can also buy lottery tickets every day, too. The goal with any business development activity is to hedge your bets by being smart and focused in your approach. Here are a few ideas to help you find the best audience and venue to speak:

• Research your competition to see where they are speaking.
• Speak to other lawyers who regularly speak to find the best venues.

• Define a niche that no one else is speaking in and leverage it to get better gigs.

• Make a list of associations, groups and settings that make sense for you and call the leader to discuss a speaking opportunity.

• Create your own venue at your firm and invite your own clients and strategic partners to hear you speak. Have them bring their friends.

Tip No. 2: Develop a plan to ensure steps aren't skipped
One of the worst feelings a lawyer can have is investing a ton of time and energy into a marketing effort and watching it fail. Sometimes you know it's a bomb right away, other times you don't know until months later.

The reason most goals aren't met is because there was never a goal to start with. Think about it.

When the Olympics begin, do you think these athletes don't have a plan? What they eat, how they sleep, where they practice and who their coach is are all elements of winning. Jumping into the speaking circuit or continuing without the results you desire is simply not acceptable.

Developing a plan can be easy if you follow a few simple steps:

• As mentioned before, you must find the right audience and setting. Make a list of targets and contact them.

• Think about what you need to get together before speaking. This might include a solid slide presentation that's interactive, collateral material that includes your contact info or a survey that will be completed at the end of the program. This should ask each participant if he or she would like to have a more in-depth business discussion with you.

• How are you interacting with the audience? Don't read your bullet points! Tell stories and share analogies that connect with the people attending. Try to make the presentation entertaining as well as educational.

• Have a follow-up plan. It's too easy to collect cards or surveys and stack them on your desk for a week or a month. This is the single greatest killer of opportunities. These prospective clients must be called within 48 hours of your presentation, while they're still remembering how impressed they were with you. Don't miss this step!

Tip No. 3: Practice doesn't make perfect. Perfect practice makes perfect.

Have you ever heard that before? It's true and I can prove it. I was on the driving range two weeks ago practicing my golf swing. I hit a bucket of balls and then I went out to play a round of golf. The next week I did the same thing again. Have I gotten better from this practice? Of course not! The reason my game doesn't improve is that I'm practicing the same bad habits and swing every week.

When trying to get higher level speaking gigs, it's important to be regarded as one of the best. Not only do people understand your level of expertise, you become more desirable as a speaker. This means bigger and better opportunities to speak to the audiences that you want.

The best way to accomplish this feat is to improve your speaking skills. Again, reading your PowerPoint slides or speaking monotone to a group just isn't going to cut it. You need to be prepared with your content, practice it and then make improvements before speaking again.

I once had a presentation in front of a law firm of about 50 attorneys. At the end of the program, one of the attorneys approached me to compliment me on the presentation. It seemed a bit unusual, but he mentioned that he was tracking how many times I said "um" during my 75-minute presentation. Weird, right?

To me, this was an amazing compliment because years ago my speeches were littered with "ums" and "uhs." This was one of those practice and improve moments that I had after watching video of myself speaking. Back then I counted more than 40 "ums" and "uhs."

Regardless of your area of practice or years as a lawyer, you can make it as a speaker if you find the right subject, the right audience and if you work to improve your performance as you go.

Many of my clients excel at speaking because they've fixed the recurring issues that held them back. While speaking is rarely a quick fix for developing a bigger book of business, it can be a long-term strategy that changes the game for you.

CHAPTER 10

EFFECTIVE TIME MANAGEMENT FOR LAWYERS: IS IT REALLY POSSIBLE?

As a coach working exclusively with attorneys, no one understands the stress and demands placed on a legal practitioner better than I do.

Sometimes it feels like my entire day revolves around the demands being placed on lawyer's time. Not to mention the additional stress that's created when we discuss investing time in business development. It makes perfect sense why most attorneys shy away from their marketing activities.

Time challenges aside, you must know by now that nothing will have a greater impact on your personal and financial freedom than having your own book of business.

Therefore, it's never been more important to effectively manage your time to ensure you can fit in the billable hours and do business development as well. By the way, it sure would be nice to see your family, too! Here are three tips to help you improve the balance in your practice to create the career you've been dreaming of.

Time Tip 1: Have a solid plan for business development.

Other than doing nothing, the worst thing you can do as a lawyer is to approach business development in a haphazard fashion. Attending events, writing articles or even speaking can be ineffective if your audience isn't aligned with your goals.

You need to have a plan in writing to ensure you are spending your time in the right places with the right people. Think about the types of legal buyers and strategic partners you need to meet. Ask yourself, where do they spend their time? How do I get in front of them? How many do I need to build relationships with to really grow my book?

A good plan should lay out your goals, strategies and tactics to accomplish your objectives in the fastest time possible. Think of the plan as a car GPS. Before we had this tool, we would drive miles out of our way before turning around or heaven forbid ask for directions. Now the GPS tells us when we made a bad turn and how to get back on track. This is what a good plan will do for you.

Time Tip 2: Use your calendar to schedule time for business development.
You schedule meetings for a closing, deposition or a trial, then why not schedule time for business development. They are all important and need to get done, so treat them with equal importance.

Based on where you are in your career, how much time you need to carve out and your goals to grow your book, there needs to be an emphasis on carving out time daily or weekly for business development.

Here are three thoughts and best practices to think about:

• Look at your calendar to find times when you are less likely to be distracted by e-mail, phone calls or other people in your office. Not to boast, but I get into my office three days a week at 6 a.m. This gives me a solid six hours a week when I can get e-mails out, leave voice mails or make contacts through LinkedIn. If you're a night owl, that might be better for you.

• Once you do get meetings on your calendar, be sure to use the meeting invite tool to ensure that these meeting stick. Changing schedules and cancellations are sometime inevitable, however, we can curtail them slightly by getting into someone's calendar at once. If you're not sure how to use this tool, ask the person in the office next to you. It's become as popular as e-mailing.

• Use your calendar to schedule everything! If you have to make a call, write an e-mail or follow up with someone, schedule it. As I mentioned earlier, you need to start treating your marketing activities the same way you treat the law.

Think of your schedule like an advanced to-do list. The more you use your calendar to schedule things, the more you will actually do. Just seeing a follow-up call pop up on your screen will prompt you to follow through.

Time Tip 3: Always pick the low-hanging fruit first.
With all of the networking groups, associations and coffee meetings to choose from, you may quickly find your time drained away from you. One of the first things I suggest to attorneys is to look closely at their network and find the easiest way to obtain new business.

This might include meeting with existing clients to cross-sell, up-sell or find quality introductions. There might also be some family or friends who are in power positions, but haven't been properly tapped into yet. Whatever the situation, it's critical to leverage these contacts first.

A few concerns that you might have with this approach is the possibility of "blowing" the opportunity or "disrupting" the relationship. While this is always a remote possibility, here are some soft and gentle approaches that might ease your mind when venturing into uncharted territory:

• Be curious. You're a lawyer right? Use that as your excuse to ask a thousand questions about this person's business. Everyone has goals and challenges that they're more than happy to share with you.

Just be a great listener and ask open-ended questions to uncover possible needs. Then it might be more natural to discuss your value or services. By the way, "value" might be discussing the law in your office over coffee or referring them to someone else who can help solve a problem. Either way, you will have a much better idea of the opportunity for you to do business now or in the future.

An example of this would be at a family function where you see Uncle Dan every year. He owns a $20 million website company. You can ask him, "What do you love about your business?" and "What types of challenges do you have running a company of that size?"

Once you start Uncle Dan talking about his favorite subject, himself and his business, you can keep asking deeper questions to identify a possible need or a question he might have for you on the legal side.

• Ask for advice. In this scenario, you are looking to better understand the mindset of a business owner or general counsel. Ask some great questions to obtain their advice and help. It's then possible that they might try to help you with your goals, make an introduction to someone they know or allow you to share your knowledge to help with a problem within their own company.

• Look to obtain an introduction from an existing client. Look, you're good at what you do and your client is happy. In addition, you've invested time taking her to lunch, a game, golfing, etc. Maybe it's time to ask for a high-level introduction to someone in her network that might want to have a similar experience.

It might make sense to schedule a lunch with your client, and before getting off the call say, "I'm looking forward to our lunch on Friday. I have a favor to ask that would be really meaningful to me. I know you are well-connected and have been happy with my work. Would you be open to introducing me to one or two of your business associates?"

This type of question is permission-based and should be received positively. The worst that can happen is that she will say "no." The best thing can be an introduction to a new client that could make your year. Plus, if she does say "no," it might be a wake-up call that you might need to work on your relationship building skills.

One way or another, you have to get your time under control. Remember, no one ever said on their death bed, "If only I had billed a few more hours." You can create a more focused and balanced approach to your practice by creating a plan, better utilizing your calendar and focusing on the low-hanging fruit.

CHAPTER 11

HOW TO GET YOUR NEW YEAR OFF TO A SUCCESSFUL START WITH 10 TIPS TO FOLLOW

When a year is fading in your rearview mirror, you may be asking yourself what needs to change to improve your marketing efforts in the new year.

In my experience, the key to success in business development is evaluating what you did both well and not so well this past year, and make some substantive changes to the not so well.

To help you with this, here's my business development best practices top 10 list for a new year. If you can execute on even two of these, it might make the difference for the coming year. Good luck!

Tip 1: Write a BD plan!
It might not sound like a tough ask, but 95 percent of all attorneys don't have a solid plan for growing their book of business. Without a plan, you may be all over the place with your BD activities.

Try defining your growth as it relates to new originations or number of new clients you would like to add. Then create two to four strategies or activities that will be a good use of your time.

For example, contact existing clients or other lawyers for referrals versus attending random networking events. Try to invest time where the low hanging fruit is. Lastly, develop some actionable tactics to accomplish each strategy. This type of plan will be your GPS for the year. Be sure to track your activity to see what's working and what is not.

Tip 2: Get your LinkedIn up to speed.
I know, I know, LinkedIn is social media and who wants to get involved in that for business? You need to! Like it or not, this is your online resume for business that may be coming your way. Having a solid profile will help solidify your skills and expertise in your area of practice as well as building your personal brand.

Take 30 minutes and clean it up. Having a professional photo, expanded summaries and adding your blog articles will help to get you found.

Tip 3: Develop a client retention plan.
How do you keep your clients happy, loyal and committed to your partnership in business? Is this something you're doing haphazardly? Most attorneys do not have anything in place to ensure that they keep their clients close and happy.

My suggestion is to break your clients into A, B and C groups. Make the A's really happy by scheduling time with them monthly or quarterly. Schedule time to send them articles and provide "counselor" type of advice beyond the matters you work on for them. Maybe even find new business or contacts for them. My point, go way beyond the call of duty. Then lower the bar for your B's and even lower for your C's. That's OK, because you only have so much time, right?

Tip 4: Get organized with your time.
I'll keep this short. Time is money! The idea that you haven't read or studied how to be efficient with your time is crazy. Go online right now and buy the book "Getting Things Done" by David Allen. Read this over the break and follow it to position yourself to succeed in the new year.

Tip 5: Find the hot topic in your space and work it!
Think about how a crazy year impacts your space and leverage it with speaking and writing.

Are you an employment attorney? How about an article on do's and don'ts in the workplace. If you're a tax attorney, how about a presentation on the political climate and what that means for midmarket businesses.

Try to get ahead of things to be the first one talking or writing on new subjects. While most attorneys know this, few actually execute on it. Hmm ...

Tip 6: Create originations through cross-marketing.
For those of you in small, midmarket or large law firms, this is the no-brainer of the century. Create new business for the firm, get origination credit, while not having to do any of the work. Nice!

Commit to building relationships with three different partners who you can trust to refer business to. Then, when you're meeting with your clients and strategic partners, ask questions that might open doors for your partners. For example, if you're a litigator working with a CEO in the midmarket, ask about the company and see if there are employee issues. This might be a setup for your labor and employment partner. If you don't ask questions, don't expect to be referred in.

Tip 7: Stop pitching, selling and solving.
In my first book, "Sales-Free Selling," I teach the art of selling, without selling. This means we need to improve our asking, listening and empathy skills. The key to successfully closing more business is by allowing the client to buy into you, versus you selling yourself to him.

The next time you hear a legal problem that you can solve through talking, stop yourself. Take a few more minutes to ask detailed questions and learn what the real pain points are for this prospective client. Here's a good mantra to follow: "prescription before diagnosis is malpractice."

Tip 8: Be "the curious attorney."
When meeting with friends and family for the holidays, do a better job of asking questions about their jobs and businesses. If you can stay curious, you may find opportunities to help solve a business or legal problem.

You might say, "How's business?" Or, "What's new in the widget business these days?" Now listen. Then, once he's shared something with you, ask, "Tell me more about that?" The point is to ask, listen and be curious by going deeper. If you can uncover a problem, there might be an opportunity to help solve it.

Tip 9: Develop two or three new referral sources.

Again, you may know this already, but have you taken stock recently of your existing strategic partners and how they did for you this year? Just because you like someone and they referred you business last year doesn't mean she is on board with you for next year. Take 30 minutes and review your referral sources to determine where your business came from this year. Who was hot? Who was not?

If a few of your best and brightest have let you down, there are two simple options. First, reconnect and work together to get things back on track. Or, drop her like a sack of potatoes and find someone new to refer and get referrals from. By adding or replacing two or three referrals partners in the new year, you will have better success in your BD efforts.

Tip 10: Sorry to tell you, you might be an entrepreneur.

As the legal landscape changes and the emphasis becomes more and more about originations, you may find yourself behind in these skills. Make it a point in the new year to think of yourself in a more entrepreneurial way.

Focus on creating or building your own client base. Relying on others for work is so 2008, and we know what happened back then.

Develop better habits around business development to engage in something positive every week. In addition to building your BD plan (Tip No. 1 in case you missed it) and scheduling time, be sure to read, watch or engage in BD learning regularly. All entrepreneurs do this and you need to as well.

CHAPTER 12

CROSS-MARKETING YOUR LEGAL PRACTICE: SOME POINTERS TO FOLLOW

One of the smartest moves you can make as an attorney is to cross-market. While the concept may seem easy to digest, many attorneys struggle with implementation when meeting with existing clients. The idea here is to deliver additional services to a client beyond the one service you are currently providing.

Here's a scenario for you:

• You have a banking client and have been working on a litigation matter with her for over the past two years.

• Your relationship is solid, and you've been doing great work.

• This client has legal work far beyond the matter you are working on, however, none of this work is being given to you.

Why is that? The reasons may include:

• The client doesn't know that your firm handles other types of legal work.

• The client wasn't asked questions about the bank's business as a whole.

• The client has never met any of your partners who are highly skilled in these other areas.

• You never felt comfortable asking the client for additional work.

Whatever the reason, it's important to understand the value of cross-marketing and how it benefits everyone involved. One of the single greatest opportunities you have is the ability to bring in work and not have to actually do the work. While there are some potential downsides to this, with the right partners in place it can be a home run for you in building your book.

The main benefit to your client would be twofold. First, you would be the quarterback for your client in handling their broader legal needs. It's always best to have one person leading the charge. Second, you client's external communication would improve. Dealing with one person and one firm leads to better coordination of legal services.

What I hear on a regular basis as a business development coach for attorneys is that there is a lack of process and effective language to execute on the cross-marketing opportunities that do exist. My goal for this chapter is to provide you a tactical approach to cross-marketing in a non-salesy way. There are three steps to accomplish this task.

Set yourself up for success

Prior to meeting with an existing client, call her to set the stage for your meeting. Let her know that in addition to catching up on the matter at hand, you would like to discuss her business as a whole and make sure that she is limiting her legal risk.

You could say, "Lately, I've been speaking with a number of my clients who have businesses similar to yours. Like you, they are all happy with my litigation work, however, there were other areas within their businesses where they weren't being properly protected from a legal vantage point. If it's alright with you, I'd like to run through a proactive legal checklist with you when we get together."

The idea here is to set up the conversation ahead of time to ensure you are not springing this on your client in the meeting. You bring up the subject as "other client's issues" so you are not specifically saying that your client has these problems and therefore not insinuating directly that she has specific legal issues or needs.

This approach is also permission-based, so you are confirming buy-in from your client on this specific discussion prior to the meeting happening.

Develop your six pillars and survey questions for your client

While there are a variety of practice areas that your firm may represent, it's important to think about the top six legal pillars that are most likely to carry weight with your business clients. The six that we see on a regular basis include:

- Labor and employment
- Intellectual property
- Estate planning and succession planning
- Real estate and construction
- Litigation and dispute resolution
- Business and finance

It is important to think about each client's business and to develop your own list of six pillars as the foundation for questioning. Once you have six pillars selected, work to develop one to two primary questions around each pillar that would engage your client into dialogue around that particular area of his or her business.

Feel free to start with some general "softball" questions like, "How's your business coming along?" or "What are some of the business issues that you dealt with this past year?"

Once you have a better lay of the land, feel free to get more specific to the six pillars. If you know that your client has a number of real estate holdings, for example, you might say "I know you have real estate all over the Midwest, tell me how that's coming along?" or "I know you've been expanding your real estate holdings over the past three years. Tell me about your future plans over the next three years."

Once your client has given you more information about his or her real estate needs or issues, ask a deeper question to open up the subject further. You could say, "It sounds like your growth is exponential. Describe some of the issues that occur with this type of growth," or "Who is handling this for you, and how is that coming along?"

The key here is to get your client talking about other areas of his or her business. Based on your initial questions and the follow-up ones, you may be able to uncover a business or legal problem that you could help him or her with. Try to use open-ended questions to avoid a yes-or-no response.

If you are truly interested in obtaining more business from cross-marketing, take the time to write down your six main pillars and the questions that you would want to ask.

This survey could be the best tool you've ever used to develop new business. Statistically, it's much easier to obtain additional work from an existing client rather than finding new business.

Follow up

Once you've reviewed your survey with your client, it's important to secure a next step. If you found out that she wasn't 100 percent happy with her existing real estate attorney, you would want to set up a meeting with the best real estate attorney in your office.

Be sure this is someone you like and trust. Having skillful and trustworthy partners to introduce to your client can make the world of difference in effectively cross-marketing your clients.

If you're going to share your coveted client with one of your peers, be sure he is not going to steal your client down the road. To assist with this, be sure to set yourself up as the quarterback for all your client's legal needs. This will help ensure her relationship will remain strongest with you.

One of most important tactics to remember when meeting a client for cross-marketing is to never leave a meeting without a specific next step. Discuss the details with your client and include a date and time to speak or meet again.

Try to avoid saying things like, "Let's touch base in a few weeks to discuss this further." This is bad form. She is busy, and you are certainly busy. Not setting up a specific next step is asking for trouble in driving this new business forward.

Almost everyone has a calendar directly on their phone, so ask your client to schedule a follow-up meeting right there on the spot. It's not unusual to do that anymore.

The impact that cross-marketing can have on your practice is incredible. The keys to success here are to set up the meeting with no surprises, be prepared to ask questions around a variety of practice areas and to follow up right away to ensure the opportunity doesn't disappear before your eyes.

A safe idea is to try an initial run with a client that you are very close with. Explain that you have their best interests at heart and want to make sure he or she is well-protected in his or her business. Once you see how easy it is to bring in new business through cross-marketing, you will make this a priority in your business development activities moving forward.

CHAPTER 13

HOW TO PRIME THE BUSINESS PUMP: TEAMING WITH PARTNERS GOOD FOR ALL

In the previous chapter I explain the importance of cross-marketing legal services as a value-add for your existing clients.

For this next chapter, I've identified a few additional pointers that I believe round out the conversation and help you get real traction in the very important area of business development.

There are three key components to success when trying to proactively cross-market your firm.

No. 1: Know what your firm does and who you feel comfortable referring.
Before running out to cross-sell your firm, stop and think for a minute. What practice areas do we do that are most closely related to my practice area?

If you are an estate planning attorney, for example, wouldn't the obvious cross-marketing opportunity be with your tax group, real estate group or family law group? While you should be open to all practice areas, there may be a few that are more on the nose. As an estate planner, you are just less likely to run into class action, IP or big PI cases than other attorneys.

Once you've determined what areas to focus on, search out and meet with the attorneys you may be sharing clients with.

Now, some of the grumbles I hear from attorneys about cross-marketing relates to a few potential pitfalls that may occur during the process.

For example, giving a matter to your partner who, unbeknownst to you, may do a lousy job or poorly communicate with clients. Another concern might be your partner potentially stealing your client away from you.

Now, while these things happen from time to time, your first job before focusing on the cross-sell is to really vet the lawyers with whom you will be bringing in on your client deals.

If you know your partner very well and have observed how professionally and skillfully she works with other clients, your comfort level will go way up.

If you are meeting with new partners, get to know them on a personal level as well as professional. I had a business associate years ago that would talk negatively about others while we were having lunch. Not very trustworthy, so that relationship ended quickly.

The key is to meet with and qualify the partners that you believe will make you look good to your clients, while also mitigating the risk of having issues down the road.

No. 2: Get prepared with the right questions before meeting with your clients.

Congratulations on selecting a few solid partners to bring in to meet with your clients. You're ready to move onto the next step, which involves getting a list of questions prepared for your next client lunch meeting.

These questions will be critical to identifying opportunities for more work, without having to ask for it. Yes, you heard me right. You don't have to ask for the work. By asking questions and identifying areas of issue, your client will ask you for help! Nice, right?

To help you along with that process, here are a number of questions that you could ask during a lunch meeting to uncover potential business.

General litigation

• In business cash is king. How are you doing with collections and receivables?

• How are relationships with your vendors? Are they living up to their commitments to help your business succeed?

• How do you use noncompete agreements?

• How does your business protect confidentiality and long-term customer relationships?

Estate planning

• When was the last time you had your estate plan reviewed?

• What do you think would happen to your assets, including your business, if you were to die without having an estate plan in place?

- When was your estate plan drafted? Any recent changes in your family?
- How are you going to transition the business when you retire? Does your plan include an asset protection plan?

General corporate

- Is your corporate book up to date so that your business does not lose its limited liability?
- Are you expecting any transactions that will impact the business and you personally?
- Do you have issues regarding employees, vendors or customers?
- Do you have a succession plan for the business?
- Do you and your partners have a shareholder or buy-sell agreement in place?

Labor and employment

- When was the last time your company handbook was reviewed?
- Do you have restrictive covenant agreements, or do you have a need for such agreements?
- Do you have any plans to hire or fire any employees in the near future?
- Any big changes to grow or reduce your labor force this year or in the next few?
- Do you have an employee incentive plan?

Family law

- How's your family? Everyone getting along all right?
- Any changes to your family dynamics?

• Between the business and family, there are usually a number of pressure points. Where are you finding the most stress?

Real estate

• I know that you are working to grow every year. Any expansions to your space or location?

• Do you have real estate holdings and how are they doing for you?

• Are you in a lease and when is it coming up for renewal?

Intellectual property

• How do you protect your name and signature products from being copied?

• Have you estimated the value of your intellectual property in the last few years?

• I noticed that you don't have a trademark stamp on your logo. Do you own the federal trademark on your brand?

No. 3: Execute on the right approach to successfully help your clients.

As mentioned earlier, the key is to focus on the areas that are closely connected to the work you currently are doing for your client. The questions above can be started just by asking about your client's business. A normal question would be, how are things going? Or try, what's the game plan for the next year to grow the business? Or, what are some of the challenges you are having this year?

The key is to be super interested and curious. Come prepared with a number of questions that might lead to identifying the legal or business risks she might be having. Once you've got her talking, keep digging.

For instance, if she mentions that things are great, but these darn suppliers are giving her the runaround, there may be some potential contract work or collections. If she admits that there's no employee handbook in place, you may want to ask about their turnover or risk for lawsuits.

Once you've identified a new matter, try your best not to solve it yourself. The whole idea behind cross-marketing is to bring your client to the table with the expert, which isn't you.

Just get all the details together, recap the problem or need for your client and tell her, "As it turns out, Barbara, we have one of the best tax attorneys in Illinois who I know can help you with this issue. Let me set up a meeting for the three of us and we can work this out with him." That's it!

As her attorney, she trusts you to help avoid the risks and hazards associated with growing her business. This meeting does exactly that and also helps you generate more work for the firm. As the client's one-stop shop, you will be able to help ensure the service and work product is quality while also making it very hard for the client to leave. Edging out the competition has never been more important than today.

So, let's wrap this up and put a bow on it. You have to get to really know, like and trust the partners you will be referring your clients. Then, you must begin scheduling meetings with your clients to ask questions and identify new legal opportunities or ways to help.

Lastly, you should be following through to introduce your client to your partner to drive the new matter into the firm.

Follow these guidelines and you will drive more business. The best part? You generate more originations and not necessarily more work for yourself. Win-win!

CHAPTER 14

RETAINING CLIENTS DOESN'T JUST HAPPEN; COME UP WITH A PLAN AND FOLLOW IT

In the Declaration of Independence it states that "all men are created equal." While this may apply to how we treat others with respect and dignity, we can choose to be more selective with whom we invest our valuable time.

For the purpose of running a successful law practice, all clients are not created equal. As a lawyer, a critical element to running a fruitful practice is managing your time in an efficient manner. How and where you invest your time can make all the difference.

Imagine that you're standing in front of an apple tree, which is loaded with fresh apples. Some of these apples are literally right in front of your face, while others are way up high in the tree. For the sake of efficiency, which apples do you go after first? The lower apples may seem like an obvious choice, however, many attorneys are still working entirely too hard climbing ladders reaching for those apples in the tree's upper reaches.

When discussing low-hanging fruit with my attorney clients, I always start with a discussion of their existing clients. Our goal is to uncover opportunities, which will produce the highest possible value for the time invested.

As we all know, before you can begin selecting apples you must first plant the seeds and water the trees. As this relates to leveraging existing clients, there is a myth that must be eradicated first. The myth is simple: if you service your client properly, they will be loyal to you. If you believe this for even a moment, welcome back to the 1980s!

Times have changed and so must you in the way you manage your client relationships. Statistically, it's six times more work and energy to find a new client rather than to keep an existing one. That being said, we all have to step up our game to insure that client loyalty is developed with intent. One of the best ways to accomplish this is to develop a client retention and loyalty plan.

Before groaning at the idea of writing a plan, I assure you this shouldn't take more than an hour to accomplish and can make the difference between success and failure in maintaining and building your law practice.

Here are the three important elements of a client retention and loyalty plan:

Step 1: Develop a list of your key clients and rank them as an "A, B or C" client. As I stated earlier, all clients are not created equal, so be careful in how you rate these folks. I suggest three qualifiers for determining what makes up an A, B or C client.

Ask yourself questions about each client and be honest.

• How good is my relationship?

• Is this a relationship that I can develop and expand?

• Are we friends socially or is our relationship more transactional in nature?

• Does she call me for general business advice or just about the deals?

• Have I helped my client in ways beyond providing legal advice?

Next, try to determine how much opportunity the client has to grow or how connected this client may be.

• Does she have a solid network of decision-makers that she can introduce me to?

• Is her company growing and expanding?

• Are there opportunities to cross-market and share work with my partners?

The last factor in determining who to invest the most time with relates directly to the amount each client has invested with you and your like or dislike of this client.

• Does this client invest a significant amount of dollars with you or did they invest almost nothing a few years ago?

• Was this client a complete nightmare to deal with?

• Did the client cost my firm money due to poor follow-through?

• Did the client continually question and argue my rate?

Based on these three factors and any others that you believe to be important, invest 20 minutes to create a master list of your top A, B and C clients so that you can move on with Step 2 of this plan.

Step 2: What you are going to do here is to develop a list of contact and relationship building points to help ensure that we are investing the right amount of time with the right clients. Based on their ranking, you are going to do more for the high-ranked clients and less for the lower-ranked clients.

To be clear, if you have a B that you want to make an A then be sure to increase the amount of touch points with that specific client.

Here are a few examples of different touch points that you can use to develop stronger and stickier relationships:

• Schedule a lunch or coffee meeting with your client.

• Go out for drinks and get to know one another better.

• Send a card on her birthday and for the holidays.

• Take your client to a game or concert. (It's important to know what she's into.)

• Call your client to see how you can help her business.

• E-mail or call your client to congratulate her on something she's accomplished (business or personally).

• E-mail your client with an article that is relevant to her business. (You can use RSS feeds for this. Look it up.)

• Invite your client to a firm event or another high-level networking event.

• Be a resource for your client. Find her a new vendor, strategic partner or an actual new client.

Use these ideas as a guideline to create your A column, where a number of these type activities would be used. The B's would receive less contact and the C's less again.

For example, you might want to have lunch with your A clients four times a year, call each one monthly, e-mail each one monthly and find a solid contact for her twice a year. Again, the B clients would get less of your attention and time, unless you want to make that client an A-lister.

These are just a few of the many things you can do to stay in constant contact and help ensure longevity with your clients. The side effect of this activity will be to open up more doors for additional business and much needed referrals.

The stronger the relationship becomes, the less likely it is that a client will leave over price and the more open to referrals she will become.

Step 3: Scheduling time to execute on your plan is paramount to your success. While it's great to set up a plan like this, it's not worth the paper it's written on if you don't implement it. My best suggestion here is to find 30 to 60 minutes a week and schedule time as "client loyalty and development time."

Without making the time and setting it aside it will never happen for you. There will always be work and distractions keeping you from this important task. Look at your calendar and find a spot weekly where you are least likely to be distracted or busy. You can even do some of this work on the train, in the evenings or on the weekends.

If you had to choose between retaining and developing relationships that already exist and have potential for growth or attending a local networking event and maybe meeting someone of interest, which is a better use of your valuable time?

There may be value in both activities, however, the later will bear fruit much more quickly when you've followed your plan.

CHAPTER 15

LEARNING HOW TO BE A RAINMAKER: YOU, TOO, CAN BECOME A MARKETING PRO

One of the greatest challenges for any attorney in growing a book of business is the genuine discomfort of asking for business from friends, family and clients.

Reasons for this may include:

• Fear of rejection.

• The impression of being too "salesy."

• The mindset that you wouldn't want someone asking you for something.

Sound about right?

One of the best ways to get on track as it relates to growing your book of business is to leverage the low hanging fruit that is all around you.

The best way to do this is by focusing on your best contacts and using some specific language to help you overcome the "head-trash" that you may be experiencing.

Scripting out a few words before making a call like this may be the difference between obtaining five new clients this year or none at all.

By the way, waiting for the phone to ring is not an effective and proactive strategy to growing your book.

Here are a few scripts that have been very successful for my clients to assist in obtaining new business from a friend, family member, referral source and even a successful client. These scripts can be used to set up the meeting beforehand or during the meeting.

The key to success with these scripts is to:
• Make the script a part of the conversation.
• Make sure the script is used in a conversational manner.
• The script should be permission based.
• Be sure to adjust and adapt each script to your own personality and style.

Script No. 1. A friend with whom you've never discussed business before:
"I was thinking that we haven't really had the opportunity to discuss our businesses with one another and it might be valuable to learn more about what each other does as new issues come across our desks. Would you be open to a lunch where we learn more about one another and see if there are synergies?"

Script No. 2. A longtime family member with whom you've never discussed business before:
"I'd love the opportunity to grab a coffee or lunch with you in the next week or two. We see each other every year, however, I don't really know a great deal about what you do. I'd love to learn more about your business and see how I can be a resource for you moving forward. I'd also enjoy sharing a little about what I do, as I know you run into people

regularly with legal concerns. Are you free on ... [provide specific dates]."

Script No. 3. A lawyer or past referral source who you believe may have business for you:
"In addition to catching up next week when we meet for lunch, I'd like to share some possible contacts with you that might be beneficial to your business. I've been really focused lately on helping people who have helped me in the past. I'd also like to pick your brain for ideas on contacts that might make sense for what I'm doing. Is that OK with you?"

Script No. 4. A "happy" past or existing client who is well connected, but not currently offering you referrals:
"Before we meet on [date], I thought it might be helpful to think of some business connections that might be good for one another. As you know, I'm looking to meet (name a specific type of prospective client). If you're open to it, let's come up with a few names prior to meeting, that way we can both get more value from our time together."

Or

"I know you've been very happy with the work I've done over the past few years and I was thinking that you may know other business owners who would appreciate the high-level work I perform. Would you be open to discussing a few contacts with me when we meet for lunch next week? It would be really meaningful to me."

Or

"There's something I'd like to ask of you and it goes outside of my comfort zone a little, but it's important to me. I know how well connected you are and I was hoping that you'd be open to discussing some possible connections with me during our lunch next week. Is that something we can chat about?"

While there are many ways to approach the people you know for introductions, my clients have found that success happens when you try the scripts and begin to see results from your efforts.

Lawyers are always searching for proof and validation. Once you've been successful doing this a few times, your confidence will skyrocket and you'll make this a part of your marketing efforts every year.

CHAPTER 16

HOW TO BRING IN MORE BUSINESS AND AVOID BEING THAT FLASHY SALESMAN

When it comes to selling legal services, attorneys have a unique set of problems. Unlike traditional salespeople, most attorneys never wanted anything to do with sales.

You probably can't imagine yourself in law school saying, "Gee, I can't wait to graduate so I can start selling legal services!" It's just not in the genetic makeup for most legal practitioners.

While there is an inherent struggle that I witness every day in working with attorneys, there are three core issues that attorneys have that make business building very challenging.

Problem No. 1

The first big problem that attorneys need to overcome is what I call, "head trash." These are the fears and uncertainties that clog an attorney's brain as it relates to business development.

Most of us don't like dealing with salespeople and certainly never want to be seen as one. So why would you put yourself into that position?

The key to success here is to think of yourself as the top expert in your field. If someone needed a legal problem to be solved, you would be the best choice to call. Now think about all of the prospective clients in the marketplace who aren't happy with their legal representation, are overpaying or may not even realize they have a legal problem.

If you're not in front of them, they may not be getting the best. The key to removing the trash between your ears is by focusing on the buyers needs and not focusing on the pitch or the close. Shift your focus to the buyer and let them talk — while you listen. Be a good interviewer and uncover compelling reasons for them to work with you.

While this might be easier said than done, it's a critical point to being chosen. Buyers want to feel listened to and understood, not pitched or sold. Think about the buyer from this point of view and I guarantee it will help you relax and enjoy the process of business development.

Problem No. 2
The second big sales issue that attorneys have is time management. While this is not unique only to lawyers, it is one of their greatest challenges. For most attorneys, the pressure to bill hours is overwhelming. In some cases, one attorney might bill 1,800 to 2,500 hours a year. If we do the math, where is the time for learning business development, let alone executing on it?

There are two possible solutions to this problem. The first is to work harder. The second is to work smarter. You probably guessed that the second way is the right way. Fortunately, there are time management guidelines that have been developed to allow busy professionals to increase their efficiency.

David Allen, the writer of "Getting Things Done," has been preaching these strategies for years, but mainly on deaf ears.

One of his main talking points is the importance of having a process for managing your time. No one ever said that "winging it" was a good strategy to be efficient.

One of Allen's mantras is the concept of the four D's. By taking information and plugging it into one of these categories, you can make better decisions about investing your time. They go something like this:

Do it: If it takes less than two minutes to accomplish, do it and get it off your plate.

Defer it: If it's over two minutes, schedule time in your calendar to accomplish the task.

Drop it: Say no to things that aren't client or prospective client related, and stop messing around online during the workday.

Delegate it: Get rid of anything you are doing that can be done for $20 to $50 an hour by someone else. Your time is worth much more than that.

Following these guidelines isn't easy, but once you start asking which D something falls under, you'll see the difference. You will discover where your inefficiencies are, and hopefully make improvements immediately.

Problem No. 3
Attorneys aren't trained to sell legal services. There are no classes in law school about selling and even the local and state bar associations frown on openly "sales-focused" content. In some cases, the only way for young lawyers to learn sales is from a strong mentor within their firm.

However, while the mentor might have the gift of gab or be a natural-born rainmaker, you are unique and probably not built for sales. For many attorneys, observing a strong originator doesn't necessarily allow you to learn processes that will work for you.

Some people are built better for business development than others. That being said, business development is a learned skill and not something anyone is simply born with.

It's important to find a sales coaching and training program to help you develop a plan with processes to achieve your goals. The alterative would be to figure it out by yourself, which can take years and cost hundreds of thousands of dollars in lost billable time and missed opportunities.

My recommendation to most attorneys would be to treat business development the same way you would learn a new language or play a new sport.

You must immerse yourself into it by finding books, videos and, most importantly, an experienced teacher who has a strong reputation for getting results for his or her clients.

Statistically, it takes 10,000 hours to become an expert at something. While we all know you don't have 10,000 hours to invest in learning business development, you might want to consider 100 hours as a launching point.

As a starting point, check out my last book entitled, "The Attorney's Networking Handbook." For most attorneys, networking inefficiently will steal away vast amounts of time because there's no process around on how to do it. This book cuts to the chase and provides tactical and actionable solutions to get results when networking. (You can order a copy on Amazon.)

While there may be hundreds of reasons why you might find business development challenging, the key is to remove that pesky head trash, work to improve your time management skills and really immerse yourself into learning business development as a part of your career.

CHAPTER 17

TWO GROWING TRENDS IN AMERICA: PLATFORM TENNIS AND LEGAL BUSINESS DEVELOPMENT

Part of being an effective marketer these days is authenticity. I'm trying to practice what I preach by sharing more about my personal life and the interests that occupy my time outside of helping attorneys with their business development efforts.

One of my pastimes or passions is a sport you may not have heard about before. And no, it's not pickleball! It's called platform tennis or also known by some as paddle tennis. It's like tennis, racquetball and ping-ping all wrapped up in one sport and then played outside during the cold Chicago winters. If you consider Chicagoans distaste for cold weather, I finally found a reason to love the cold winter months.

When I started playing this crazy sport seven years ago, I was fortunate enough to have a 10-time national champion, Howard Sipe, as my coach and mentor. Like most athletes and top rainmakers, we learn so much from the best that it's hard to fail on their advice. Being the good student that I am, I took every nugget I could from him until the well was dry. My game improved so dramatically that I became one of the best players at my club.

So, what does this have to do with legal business development and growing a law practice? Here are five lessons I learned from my hero Howard Sipe that directly relate to growing and maintaining your law practice.

Paddle lesson #1

Positioning, positioning, positioning! The key to a successful paddle game is knowing where you stand and anticipating where the ball is going to go before it gets there. It amazes me how little the top players in the game move. It almost seems like they are lazy. Trust me, they are not! In marketing your law practice, it's critical position yourself at the right firm, with the right specialty and solving the right types of problems. Be sure to look at the economy, market trends and how your clients' needs have changed.

As you know, many of the top players in law are specialists. Bob Clifford for aviation personal injury, Anita Ventrelli for high-stakes divorce or Marc Siegel for plaintiff side labor & employment. Look ahead and pick a lane where you can thrive.

Paddle lesson #2

Down the middle solves the riddle. In paddle this means don't try for crazy, low percentage shots that are tough to hit. If you play down the middle, your chance of errors diminishes greatly.

In legal marketing, sticking to the basics can get you ahead much more quickly. Focus on your existing network versus going out and meeting a ton of new people. While both may work, only one of them can get you results quickly and with less time and effort needed. Just today, I asked a happy client if I could go through her LinkedIn contacts to identify a few lawyers that may be interested in dramatic growth like she was. "Done deal," she said. Now, how hard was that? In less than five minutes of effort, I'll be speaking with one or two new lawyers I never would have met before.

Paddle lesson #3

Set up the offense. If you try to win every shot that comes your way, there is very little chance for success in this sport. It is almost exclusively a game of errors. It's simple, the less errors you make, the better chance of winning.

When looking to grow your law practice, set yourself up by planning and executing with a proven process and language. This means that winging it or swinging wildly for the fences will amount to wasted time, money and effort. Invest in yourself to learn business development, marketing, social media or effective speaking to get a greater return on your unbillable time. Having more of your own clients equates to greater control over your future in law.

Paddle lesson #4

Know your role on the court. Part of being on a team is playing with a number of different people, with different strengths and weaknesses. The best paddle teams typically have an alpha and a beta. This is important because when you put two alphas together, they will fight to control the offense at the risk of losing the match. The best partners have one of each, the beta supporting and setting up the alpha. The alpha can't easily do the job without the betas set-up skills.

The key takeaway here is look for mutual partnerships that will benefit you and your cohort, be it a colleague at your firm, a new strategic partner or even your clients. How can you add value for them and them for you? I partner with my clients to provide valuable introductions for each of them just about every week. This is in addition to the coaching and training I provide to get them to their goals and beyond. When they reciprocate, I am appreciative for the introduction and in knowing that I don't have to market as hard that month.

Paddle lesson #5

Don't run through your volleys. Paddle is a game of serving and volleying. Most novice players and even more experienced ones, like myself, miss easy volleys when we don't stop our feet to make a clean shot. Anytime I miss a volley, I check in with myself to see if I did in fact stop before making the play. I didn't. As we all know, it's all about making adjustments and not repeating bad habits.

In business development, it's clear that most lawyers don't take a moment to think about their past experiences to try and identify the gaps or areas of improvement. What a huge mistake! My attorney clients will tell you that I am all about reviewing the proverbial game tapes to find any and all missteps. We even track daily activity to see what's working or not and how this activity is converting into new business. This is a proven way to become great at something. Take one minute after your next prospective client meeting or event and see if there's anything you could have done better.

I hope you enjoyed learning a little about my favorite sport and took away a few nuggets as well. Check out "platform tennis" on YouTube to learn more about this exciting and amazing sport. I still remember years ago, as a tennis guy, looking outside in February at those idiots running around in animal cages with a hat and gloves. Boy was I the fool. Learning to do something well like paddle, or business development, can make a huge difference in your enjoyment of life and achieving your goals.

CHAPTER 18

10 TIPS TO IMPROVE YOUR ZOOM MEETINGS AND DRIVE NEW BUSINESS IN A POST-PANDEMIC WORLD

As your friendly neighborhood lawyer coach, I get the privilege of hearing excuses from attorneys on why business development growth is down. While no one can deny that things are weird and different, the main justification for slumping originations is Zoom.

Mainly, that in-person face-to-face meetings are where the magic happens. That being said, there are so many upsides to utilizing Zoom as a business tool that some can't see the forest for the tress. If I've piqued your interest, then you'll enjoy reading a few positive points on why Zoom is terrific and how you can grow business by leaning into it. Here are 10 suggestions to make Zoom work for your legal business development efforts in and after a pandemic.

Tip 1: Video meetings are far better than using the phone. Is it possible that someone was rolling their eyes at you and you never knew it? People are nicer and more professional when they have to look at you directly. It's also easier to convey non-verbal messages, like body language, which makes up 55% or more of your actual communication.

Tip 2: Have you ever traveled to London for a client meeting in the morning, followed up with two prospect meetings in Los Angles that same day, while still being home for dinner that evening with your family? Zoom takes you places now that you just couldn't acceptingly go to in yesterday's world. Utilize the tool to be EVERYWHERE!

Tip 3: Remember that general counsel that ignores your requests to grab lunch sometime soon? Would that same person be more open to a 30-minute Zoom call? So, instead of a two-hour commitment including travel, the GC is off the Zoom call in 30 minutes, making it more likely that he/she would be open to meeting. What I can guarantee is that you'll have zero chances if you don't ask. Now that I have your attention, let's get into the nuts and bolts of being more effective when on your Zoom calls.

Tip 4: Be sure to "set the stage" for your Zoom meetings to ensure success. This means having a professional and non-distracting background. Forget the virtual option, as it's weird and can take focus away from you. Also, be sure your face is framed in the camera so your facial expressions can be seen. Lastly, have a light behind your computer to brighten up your face.

Tip 5: I previously mentioned non-verbal communication. Be sure to look into the camera, versus staring at someone's face low down on the screen. I know this seems odd and hard to do but making eye contact is important in building trust and rapport. Additionally, use your hands to emphasize the points you are making. This will create a more impactful conversation or presentation for your online audience.

Tip 6:   Don't wing it! Just like with any in-person visit, you MUST do your research prior to the Zoom call to ensure success. Does this sound familiar, "Hey, how are things? Can you believe the changing weather?" Really, that's your opener? How about using the internet to find a recent post or article to comment on? Or discussing the person who introduced you? While this might sound like biz-dev 101, I'm amazed at how weak lawyers are at this simple tactic.

Tip 7:   Use the tools provided by Zoom to make your meetings more interactive. You have breakout rooms for group meetings, as well as screen sharing and annotations for presentations. Why not make the interaction with your client or prospect more action packed? These tools will be really helpful to drive the point home for the visual learners.

Tip 8: When engaging on a Zoom call, make the interaction more about the other person. In addition to building your relationships by being an active listener, you can ask more questions to obtain more information from your Zoom partner. Be prepared with open-ended questions that will drive urgency and next steps. As you know, a person's favorite subject is themselves.

Tip 9: Pay attention to your Zoom audience's attention. If you observe someone checking out their phone or looking away at other screens, you may be losing her/him. This is where all the other tips I just provided come into play. Lighting, eye contact and engaging questions will do much better than distracting backgrounds, staring down at your screen or talking endlessly about yourself.

Tip 10: Avoid Zoom fatigue yourself by taking a lot of breaks throughout your day. Consider walking around the office/house every hour or two to stretch and stay fresh. I don't know about you, but my daily meeting schedule has literally doubled since the pandemic started. Additionally, I can't recommend enough using a standing desk or standing desk converter. I have the converter which was very inexpensive and allows me to stand for half the day. My group presentations are always more engaging when I'm standing.

Well, that's just 10 of many reasons why Zoom can be your best business development tool, if you allow yourself to be optimistic about it. You must learn how to use it properly to get the desired effect. I hope you can use some of these tips as but one resource to grow your book of business and finish Q4 with much success.

CHAPTER 19

FRETZIN'S FIVE EMAIL TIPS THAT GET RESULTS FOR LAWYERS

One of the biggest time wasters in legal business development is emailing. You might have asked yourself one of the following questions:

- o Is my email too short or too long?
- o What do I say in the email to get a response?
- o How do I avoid the back and forth which saps my time away?
- o What is the appropriate follow up steps when there's no response?

Whatever the scenario, it's important to consider that emailing has the ability to make or break new opportunities, your time, and your level of frustration when you're already busy! So, here are five tips to help you get on the right path of using email more effectively when doing business development.

Email Tip 1: Don't have the entire conversation over an email.

One of the worst things I've seen as a biz-dev coach for

attorneys are the jaw-droppingly long essays that are produced by attorneys who say and give away too much, which fails to leave the door open for an actual call or meeting. A good rule of thumb is to limit your emails to two or three paragraphs–tops. If you think you're busy, do you really think someone wants to sit and read an email where they have to scroll down the page to finish it?

Try to keep the email to three core elements. For example, if you received a referral to a new potential strategic partner, open it up with a "thank you" to the introducer. Then, mention briefly why it would be good to get together (list a reason or two). Lastly, share some specific dates/times that work for you and ask your new friend which might work for her. It's okay to save your questions or pitch for later when you're meeting for lunch.

Email Tip 2: Consider the goal of the email before writing it

When I make or respond to an email, I always take a moment to consider what the end goal is before sending. Is it to get this person on the phone or schedule a face to face in the next two weeks? Email should be used as a tool to get that end result accomplished, not to actually have the conversation. Don't make the mistake of selling or dragging emails out to demonstrate expertise. Focus on the "less is more" philosophy here.

Email Tip 3: Use email to set up a "game plan" for the meeting

It's possible that you've had networking meetings that

went absolutely nowhere. One of the main reasons this happens is because no one stepped up with an agenda. A great solution for this is to share a proposed game plan by email to set the table for a successful visit. Some elements to include would be:

- o Time: Try to keep the meeting to 45-60 minutes, versus a two-hour marathon.
- o Purpose: Why are you meeting? If it's to discuss a possible new strategic partnership, you may want to share that idea.
- o Expectation: Is this to learn about one another? You might imply splitting up the talk time to ensure both parties get to learn about one another.
- o Outcome: What are you hoping to have happen here? Share the mutual intent with your new friend.

Email Tip 4: Use specific dates to remove the back and forth

As I mentioned earlier, it can be very time consuming to go back and forth with a new networking partner or prospective client to solidify a dates/time to meet or speak. The best solution for this is to always include three to five specific dates/times that work for you in the next week or two. This is much better than emailing someone and saying, "let me know when you're free?"

Providing dates that work for you allow the other person to quickly check their calendar and get back to you in ONE EMAIL with the date that works. Then, I recommend sending a meeting invite to get this meeting entered into both parties' calendars right away.

Email Tip 5: Email scripts will improve your follow up.

One of the things I help clients with regularly is scripting out follow-up emails to re-engage people who need a little push. Here are three examples:

o   Initial email to a prospective client:

Hi Karen,

It was great chatting with you today. As we discussed, it would make a lot of sense to get together and take a deeper dive into your legal issues. We can meet in my office for 45 minutes and hash out your needs. Here are some dates/times that I have available. At your earliest convenience, please let me know which works for you as my calendar evolves daily.

Thanks!

(Then, list three to five dates and times.)

o   If she doesn't respond in three to five business days, you might send her this:

Hi Karen,

I hope the day finds you well. Just checking in on a follow-up email I sent you last week. You might have missed it, which is no issues at all. I know how busy you are. That being said, my schedule has changed and I need to provide you some alternative dates/times for us to get together in the next few weeks. I know these legal issues are pressing, so please get back to me at your earliest convenience.

Thanks!

(Then, share the new dates.)

o   If she doesn't respond to the second email, then

send this one. It allows you to take back control from Karen who's been unresponsive:

Hi Karen,
Just checking in to see if everything is okay. When we spoke a few weeks ago, it seemed clear that we should get together and discuss your pressing legal needs. Has anything changed? Like you, I am extremely busy and don't want to bother you if you've changed direction or have decided this wasn't urgent as originally thought. Unless I hear from you by tomorrow, I'll go ahead and close your file. I hope the issues don't get worse and I'm happy to help you when you're ready.
(No need to provide dates here; you're just looking for a response.)

These emails escalate to generate a response to re-engage the prospective client. The last email actually works to move the prospect to a "no," which might seem counterintuitive. In reality, it's better than chasing after someone who is not being honest with you or has moved in another direction. For many of my clients, they love the closure and the time it saves them moving someone from "no response" to a "no."

As you can see, this isn't brain surgery, however, it is really important to have a little process, structure and specific language when using email for business development. I hope you can use a few of these ideas for better time management and overall results when using email.

CHAPTER 20

FINDING GOLD AS A LAWYER TAKES A MINER'S MENTALITY

Let's be honest, we all have our guilty pleasures on TV. For me, it's a reality show called Gold Rush. You might find this a little sad or you may be impressed that I know more about gold mining than just about anyone. If you were to ask (and please don't), I could find land, have the equipment built and direct a crew to pull this precious metal from the ground with significant confidence. Since I don't have "gold-fever," or the lower back for it, I think I'll stick with my true passion, helping lawyers find their own gold in business development.

If you haven't figured it out yet, this article will demonstrate my academic knowledge of gold mining and how it directly relates to growing your law practice. Here are the three lessons to gold mining including, of course, your valuable takeaways.

Gold Mining Tip 1: Don't just go where you think the gold is, always test the ground first.
When people think of gold, their minds immediately go to California, Colorado or Alaska as, historically, that is where

gold has been found. The reality, though is that much of this previously fertile ground has already been "mined-out" or was barren from the start. A smart miner will drill test holes in a few different areas to see how much gold is really there before investing time, money and energy on a claim (piece of land).

In looking for new clients, it's always best to go where you believe the business may be, with the added task of testing your options before going all in. For example, there may be a networking group you've had your eye on. To learn more, try calling the event host with some pointed questions or actually attending a "tester" event before committing to joining.

Additionally, you may have been targeting specific referral sources that haven't been panning out "pun intended," so consider updating your approach or finding new referral sources that may be better aligned with your goals today. To ensure better results you must always have the mindset to be testing and learning, versus digging on the same barren piece of land.

Gold Mining Tip 2: Are you looking for nuggets or fine gold?
When most people think about gold mining, they have imagery of quarter-sized nuggets glimmering up from the gold pan. In reality, these nuggets are rare. Most of the gold that is mined is cleaned off the rocks and is fine like sand. When a miner puts together a sluice box (the gold trapping device), it must be clear as to which type of gold he/she is mining for. Otherwise, the miner will lose most of what there is to be caught.

In business development you must have clarity about the kinds of matters you should be focusing on bringing in. If producing million-dollar litigation matters is your thing, go after that. If ten-thousand-dollar transactional matters is more likely, keep your focus on those sized matters. If you do the work you love and do it well, your reputation and marketing efforts will bring you that big nugget you've been waiting for. In the meantime, go after the appropriate targets.

Gold Mining Tip 3: In gold mining, it's all about the team.

Sound familiar? It's one thing to find good land, and another to set up the right equipment. Without a strong team to support your efforts, it's going to be an exercise in futility. In working the land for gold, you have many elements to manage including land, water, waste and equipment that all needs constant attention. Failure with the flow of water means your rocks aren't cleaning off the gold. If the waste, or tailings, aren't cleared, you'll damage your equipment. The takeaway with this analogy is that the attention needed to run a successful mine simply cannot be overstated–or done alone.

If you're serious about developing business, you now understand the importance of having a strong team surrounding you. Here are a few important tasks that must be delegated to successfully grow your legal business:

- Remove as much administrative burden as you can. You must have a strong paralegal, personal assistant or virtual assistant to handle much of the non-legal work so you can focus on bringing in the business.

- Utilize the most up-to-date software to automate anything and everything you can. Ask you assistant to help you accomplish this.
- If you're bringing in significant work be sure to delegate to the best associate or partner possible. Without proper delegation, you're going to run out of hours. This will stall or stop your business development efforts in their tracks.
- Outsource your marketing to your assistant, your marketing team or hire virtually. Again, it's all about your time and staying out in front of people (even by Zoom).

Probably the best analogy I have is the importance of finding gold in the first place, mining it and then staying in the mine until you've recovered all that was available. No one in their right mind would find gold and never go back for the rest.

Whether your gold is podcasting, blogging, networking, golfing with referral sources or leveraging your clients for quality introductions (the best), be sure to educate yourself on business development and marketing best practices to ensure ongoing success. The gold is there–now go and find it, mine it and improve how you capture it.

CHAPTER 21

FISHING FOR NEW BUSINESS FOR YOUR LAW PRACTICE

Over the summer I enjoyed the most wonderful fish fry dinner with my family. We have this special treat each summer up at my in-law's lake house after catching walleye, perch and crappies. It's easy to tell the difference between a good fish fry and an average one by how fresh the fish is. My wife can tell by the yummy noises I make when I'm eating.

So what does this have to do with growing your law practice or building a book of business? Well, just hold your horses and let me rewind to 15 years ago when I started fishing with my father-in-law.

As everyone knows, part of the deal when you get married is the in-laws. My wife's family hails from Milwaukee, with a lake house in Fond Du Lac, Wisconsin. While I've been around fishing for most of my life, my father in-law, Sol, has been perfecting the art for over 65 years. Fishing with him this year made me think of three spot-on analogies fishing has to business development that were spot on, so I thought I would share.

Fishing Tip 1: Change things up

You don't have to be a fan of fishing to understand the concept of trial and error. When we go on the lake, Sol knows all the hot spots or reefs where the fish are most likely to be. If we try for a period of time and it's not happening for us, we try a different spot.

Now consider your efforts in business development; what's been working and what needs to be changed up. If you've given a networking group a year or two and have little to no business to show for your efforts, either change your tactics for networking, or bail on the group (nicely) and try another group. Don't feel obligated to stay longer than your original commitment if there are better or more beneficial places for you to invest your valuable time.

Fishing Tip 2: Perfect practice

A famous name amongst Wisconsinites is Vince Lombardi, who coached the Green Bay Packers from 1959-1967 (boo Packers!). One of the most famous quotes from this five-time champion was "Practice doesn't make perfect. Perfect practice makes perfect." Read that again. This goes against what we've learned our whole lives. Practicing imperfectly doesn't make perfect. You must learn and improve in order to really practice perfectly.

Now we can fast forward the 15 years I've been out on Lake Winnebago. I used to feel a nibble on my line and just yank the pole up hard to hook the fish. This past weekend, I felt the fish take the line and then I waited and waited until the fish was running away with the bait before setting the hook. In days past, I would hook one or two out of ten, while today I catch more like eight out of ten. Sol was patient in explaining to me how the fish bite and what I have to do to improve my technique. I wanted to advance my skills and was eager to learn, which is 90% of the battle.

The key take-away related to improve your business development skill is to continue learning and improving how you market, prospect and sell legal services. You can't expect a better result if you're doing the same things over and over in an ineffective way. A good example of this is in your "pitch meetings." Are you still convincing, solving and telling the prospective client why they should hire you? Or, have you practiced perfectly, learning that you should be asking, listening, empathizing, and qualifying before solving anything?

Fishing Tip 3: Learn from the best

I call Sol the fisherman savant, because he can tell what kind of fish he's caught before he even sees it. He actually feels the tug, twitch or weight on the line on his fingertips and makes the call. "It's a walleye" he'll announce to the delight of my son and me. Learning from someone who is so knowledgeable and talented about fishing has been a real blessing for me. My skills and confidence on the boat are night and day from where I started years ago.

Now it's time to ask, who's been the greatest teacher, coach or influencer in your life? Was it your basketball coach in high school or the wise mentor who headed up Labor & Employment at your firm? Learning from the best is something we all can get behind and understand.

From a business development standpoint, who are you speaking with to improve your business development skills and acumen? It's mission critical, especially with all that's going on right now, to find that extraordinary mentor, coach or teacher to take your business development to the next level. Invest time, energy and even your own hard-earned dollars to get ahead while you can. The most common phrase I hear from my clients is, "I only wish I had found you 20-years ago."

Try to use the lessons from my experiences fishing to drive improvement and change to get more out of your legal career. And if you're ever out on Lake Winnebago and see a guy drift fishing over the reefs, it might just be Sol, the best fisherman I've ever known.

CHAPTER 22

FIVE PERSONALITIES THAT SHOULD NOT HIRE A COACH

If you've been reading my "stuff" over the past five years, you know that I always try to provide valuable takeaways and tips to improve your business development. This article is going to be a little bit different, in that I'm going to help you, the reader, figure out if hiring a coach to help grow your law practice is a good idea or not.

After reading this, you should have some level of clarity on where you stand on the subject (if you've ever wondered). The easiest way to do this is to share characteristics of lawyers who will simply not be successful working with a coach. As a public service announcement, hiring a coach is a very personal decision and is not right for everyone (especially the people with the traits about to be named).

Type 1: The narcissist
If feelings of empathy and being humble escape you, you may have some narcissistic tendencies. That being said, if you do, you wouldn't admit to it anyway. People who know everything and feel the world revolves around them are not good candidates for coaching.

Working with a coach involves being vulnerable, opening up about weaknesses that are holding you back and accepting advice or ideas that might vary from your own. Generally speaking, a narcissist knows everything already. Just ask him.

Type 2: The objector

"Your Honor, I object!" Skillfully objecting in a courtroom to aggressively represent your client is one thing but may be problematic when working with a coach. If you find yourself being closed-minded and negative about most things, hiring a coach to make improvements in your life/business might be a challenge.

A way to see if there's hope for you yet is to ask yourself, "Am I an optimist or a pessimist?" If you're the latter, it may be good to surround yourself with someone positive and inspiring to help you turn a more positive corner. If you hated this last sentence, then coaching is still not for you.

Type 3: The excuse generator

Did the dog eat your homework? Did your car "break down?" Were you too busy to call back that client? One of the reasons people get value working with a coach is the accountability. However, if you are an excuse machine, you may be too broken to invest in coaching. Maybe try a psychologist.

One of the main benefits of coaching is that you have an accountability partner who can help you get stuff done. Just today I obtained a commitment from my client to send out five emails before the end of the day. The bcc's will be in my inbox by 5:30 p.m. or else! I'm not sure what "or else" is, but he's on board. N

Not knowing or understanding how to do something is fixable. Creating excuses and blowing off commitments is unacceptable. I've fired a few clients in my day for wasting my time and blowing smoke up my you know what.

Type 4: The short-sighted
Would you step over dollars to pick up pennies? Most attorneys do that every day when working to build a successful law practice. Sometimes I actually do the math with a new prospective client so he/she can understand what's at stake. Think about it, your time is literally money. It's what you're selling. Ask yourself two questions:

o   "What is my time really worth?" Some of the lawyers I've worked with invest hundreds of unproductive hours a year doing business development with little to show for it.

o   "What's the opportunity cost of missing or losing new business opportunities?" Whether you're looking for $3,500 dollar estate plans or $500,000 litigation matters, not having a proven system for locking up that business could be costing you big money every year.

o   Use this formula: P + F = T (Past $ + Future $ = Total dollars lost). It's not just the past years where you've lost business/opportunities, but the future as well.

Being short-sighted means that for years you're choosing to struggle– or just maintain– on your own. One of the key benefits to coaching is learning better processes and efficiencies that cut back on your "self-taught" learning curve.

Type 5: The penny-pincher
No joke, my 14-year-old son thinks this is me. I try to explain to him that I'm all about the value of things, but he's too young and immature to know the difference. My own family matters aside, ask yourself, "What's a good return on investment for me?" The state of the stock market at the end of 2020 was about 16% growth. Wow, pretty good. If you put in $10,000 dollars, your return would be $1,600. Not

too shabby. What about investing in your own career? What are the possibilities?

In a recent BE THAT LAWYER podcast interview with a local recruiter, he shared the difference in income between a service partner and a rainmaker with $1 million year in originations. It's staggeringly different. You must look at working on yourself as an investment greater than any other. It's all about unleashing your best self and creating best practices to live and work by.

I'll wrap up with a word of warning. All coaches, advisors and mentors are NOT created equal or may not fit your personality. You need to find a coach who is a good fit for YOU to ensure success. Be sure to properly evaluate and qualify before engaging.

A good idea is to speak with a few of their past clients to hear their stories or ask if the coach will provide a one-time coaching session to test the waters a bit. Coaching can be a game-changer for you if you DON'T possess any of the five characteristics mentioned in this piece. I can tell you from experience that I wouldn't be a successful coach today had I not invested in many top coaches for myself over the past 20 years.

CHAPTER 23

LEGAL BUSINESS DEVELOPMENT LESSONS FROM SEINFELD

I don't know about you, but I'm a huge Seinfeld fan. I've probably seen each hilarious episode four or five times. Even with the massive amount of shows being pumped out of Netflix, Amazon Prime and countless others, I haven't seen a show that literally makes me laugh out loud as much as Seinfeld (Big Bang is a close second).

So, you might be wondering, what does that have to do with business development as a lawyer? Here are five funny situations or lines from Seinfeld that I have miraculously turned into a teachable moment.

Seinfeldism 1: The Telemarketer
One of the best lines or scenes in the history of television is when Jerry gets a phone solicitation at home. We all know how annoying and disruptive they are, so we usually just screen them out or hang up immediately when they start talking. Jerry does one better. He tells a telemarketer that he's busy now but would be happy to call the solicitor later when "he's" at home. When the solicitor objects and says he doesn't want to be disturbed at home, Jerry says, "now you know how I feel" and hangs up on him. NICE!

The takeaway on the BD front is how unwanted selling, is, well, unwanted. My suggestion to all attorneys is to STOP convincing, selling and pitching. Start off on the right foot by demonstrating your expertise and differentiation in the marketplace by providing value to others through effective social media posts, videos and articles. Then, when you do have an opportunity to sell, don't do it. Focus on building relationship, asking questions, listening and empathizing with your new prospective client. You'll be amazed at how "bought in" he or she will be.

Seinfeldism 2: The Contest
If you haven't seen this episode, you are missing out on TV gold! Jerry and his gang have a contest to see who can hold out the longest... . While I'm not able to share the specifics of the contest in this "G-rated" article, feel free to look it up.

The "ah-ha" moment here is to engage your competitive mindset with others to achieve a goal or accomplishment. This could be a group or the partner in the office next to you. Have a competition on who can complete their business/marketing plan for 2021 first or who can get the bigger bonus off of new originations in 2021. Even if you're a solo, you can find another lawyer who may be willing to compete with you. Whatever the case, getting others to share in something fun and financially rewarding can't be a bad thing.

Seinfeldism 3: Yada, Yada, Yada
When George's girlfriend mentions that her ex-boyfriend was over the other night and "yada, yada, yada," she was tired the next day, he loses his mind. This is another Seinfeld gem that not only displays George's insecurities, but shows how people can gloss over the details to get to the end of the story without sharing the much-needed specifics.

This is so relevant as we leave 2020 in the rearview mirror and approach 2021 with a specific and detailed approach to growing one's law practice. Anyone can say, "I'm going to develop business in 2021 and yada, yada, yada, I'm sure I'll have my best year ever." All lawyers need to consider a written plan that outlines and details the specific actions that will lead to your best year ever. This doesn't have to be an MBA 30-page novel, but rather a two-three pager that provides direction on a daily, weekly and monthly basis. Happy to share a sample plan and explanation with you if you email me at steve@fretzin.com.

Seinfeldism 4: Elaine's Crazy Dance

I think everyone has a friend who is a terrible dancer. Maybe they know it or maybe not. In this episode, Jerry's friend Elaine is seen dancing at a work party in front of her entire staff. What she doesn't know is that she's the worst dancer EVER! Obviously, the fact that she's clueless about it makes this super funny.

The take-away here is that you might be a terrible networker and not even realize it. There are still lawyers out there pushing business cards or aggressively asking for business without any thought of reciprocation or connecting the other party. I have found that in many cases, the lawyer doesn't realize his/her skills are outdated or inappropriate. When I see a networker making these mistakes, I don't immediately discount them or toss them aside like yesterday's Amazon box. It may be possible that with a little help, support and coaching, this person could turn things around. By the way, if you're getting referrals from people without helping them in return, you might be the person I'm describing.

Seinfeldism 5: The Soup Nazi

For you Seinfeld fans, I couldn't leave you hanging. This is not only one of the best episodes, it's also so crazy and ridiculous, you'll never forget it. There's a new soup take-out joint in the neighborhood and it's the best (the best Jerry, the best!). There's only one problem. The Chef running the restaurant is very, very strict. This doesn't end well for George who asks for bread and thusly gets his soup taken away from him. "No soup for you!" exclaims the Chef.

Getting to the biz-dev takeaway, you must consider what you are willing to do to get your delicious soup or decide to go your own direction and find another great place to eat. From a legal business development point of view, there isn't only one good way to develop business. If the method you're trying isn't working, then simply try something else.

Years ago, I was in a legal networking association. I found it to be dry, isolating and clannish. It didn't take me too long to realize this wasn't going to be enjoyable or beneficial to my business, so I bounced. There are dozens of ways to grow business as a lawyer, so don't stay too long or feel there's only one avenue to go down.

My suggestion is to focus on your low-hanging fruit. Make a list of your clients, top referral sources and best friends to meet up with and selflessly help connect them. They should reciprocate with a little coaching, which may lead to easy business for you.

If you're a fan of Seinfeld, I hope you enjoyed us sharing a couple of fun moments and takeaways together. If you've never seen it, give it a try and I hope it makes your belly hurt like it does mine. Either way, make next year your best year ever through proper planning, execution and follow through.

CHAPTER 24

BUSINESS DEVELOPMENT FOR THE LAWYERS WHO HATE IT

I am sitting at a Discount Tire in Mount Prospect waiting for my car to receive four shiny new tires. The problem? My lease is up in two months. There's a bad taste in my mouth today knowing that my money is shortly going down the drain. I also need new back brakes, which just adds insult to injury.

The reason to share these complaints with you is because it's important to understand where my priorities are– the safety of my family, myself and others on the road. Protecting myself and others from an unsafe vehicle is necessary even when it seems unfair or costly.

Let's move this metaphor to the topic you know me for so well, legal business development. As you may recall from previous articles, my father practiced law for over 35 years and NEVER had to do any business development other than just being a great lawyer, which he was. That was the past and that ship has sailed. Ask any legal recruiter, "How do I change firms," and the answer will not alter. "What's your book of business?"

If you're serious about longevity and sustainability in your legal career, having your own book of business is the key. Here are the top five reasons lawyers hate doing business development and what I hear every day. Use these points to overcome those feelings that, quite frankly, may be holding you back from growing your book and even enjoying the process along the way.

Hate point #1. "Business development is a waste of time." I agree! Business development can be an incredible time suck if you don't know what you're doing. That's the equivalent of me walking into a courtroom and trying a case without a law degree or any experience in litigation. Get it together! Read a book, listen to a podcast, talk with a rainmaker you know. Do something, anything to move the needle. Sometimes just taking the first step is everything.

Hate point #2. "My firm won't give me money for learning business development." BOO-HOO! Did your firm give you money for going to law school to then come and work for them? While the firm may end up being the recipient of your rainmaking efforts, ultimately you will be the one with control over your destiny, which includes financial security and a seat at the table within your firm. Consider investing in yourself and not holding the firm responsible for your career decisions.

Hate point #3. "I'm too busy to do business development." You may be right, particularly (or especially) if you're doing everyone else's work. That being said, if you lose a big client, or your "feeder" rainmaker leaves the firm or, heaven forbid, a recession occurs (like NOW), you're in a bit of a pickle.

One of the first things I teach lawyers is time management, to ensure they can create time that didn't exist before. It's amazing what can be found when I have a client track his/her day or week. In some instances we find upwards of two hours a day that is wasted on tasks that could be delegated or done off-hours to ensure business development is a part of each day/week.

Hate point #4. "I really can't market because of COVID." That's like thinking, I can't be bothered swimming when in the middle of the ocean with sharks swimming towards you. Right now is THE time to get going on your business development efforts.

Get creative by writing for publications, speaking on Zoom events, or simply reaching out to network with other lawyers or, here's a crazy idea... your clients. There are too many uncertainties to just do nothing at this time.

Hate point #5. "Why would I want to develop business for my firm, I'm not even happy here." While that's an unfortunate scenario, it's cutting off your nose to spite your face. You may not be able to leave your firm for a different one, or even go out on your own, without having the portable book that actually allows you to make those positive decisions. I know this is a hard one but consider the importance of having your own clients that see you as their counsel. If you take care of them, they will follow you.

Whatever the self-hate talk may be around marketing your practice, consider working through these negative feelings and excuses to create your own book and successful future. Like with my tires and brakes, sometimes we have to do things that we don't want to do. As David Goggins says about mindset, "Embrace the suck," and take on the challenge head on. I hope you can, too, during these unprecedented times.

CHAPTER 25

HUNTER OR FARMER? GROW YOUR LAW PRACTICE INTO WHICH IS BEST FOR YOU

Years ago, when I was coming up the ranks as a sales professional, there were two factions that you fell into. One was as a hunter, hard charging after new business day after day. The other was as a farmer, who took care of the hunter's new client after the sale was made. Most businesspeople fell into one of these two camps. Since these definitions were created years ago, I'd like to change the paradigm to help you figure out which you are and how to more easily grow your law practice.

The new definition for a hunter is an attorney who actively pursues business development. This means you're putting yourself out there by strategically attending networking groups, meeting with clients to get more work, developing new strategic partners and other such activities.

The new classification for a farmer is a lawyer who prefers to hang back and produce content, including blogging, article writing, podcasting and social media posting.

While you might ask, "Steve, shouldn't I be doing both hunter and farmer activities?" My response would be that, of course, it's best to do both. However, for many busy attorneys I'd rather have you doing something productive rather than nothing at all. Here are three hunter and three farmer activities to select from in order to ensure that 2021 ends up better than 2020. My suggestion is to pick one to three of these and really focus on making them happen by scheduling time (like an appointment with yourself) to ensure they get done.

Hunter activity #1: Join a networking group to develop new business. Meeting new people and developing relationships is the cornerstone of a hunter's mentality. Be sure to find groups, associations, boards and clubs where you can meet potential clients or new strategic referral sources. This might sound obvious, but most attorneys aren't doing this.

Hunter activity #2: Develop a master list of all your contacts and rate them A, B or C, and then schedule time (coffee, beers, lunch or a game) with your A's and B's. These are the people you've already invested time with, including clients, other lawyers, friends and even family. It's time to see how you can help them and they can help you. An easy email to shoot out might read, "Hey Karen, I'd love to get together with you soon and catch up. I'd enjoy learning how I can add value for you in your law practice and share what's new with me. When's a good time to meet up?" Always offer to help first, as that's what networking is all about.

Hunter activity #3: Look inward at your firm for cross-marketing opportunities. You partner's already have the clients and they've never brought you in to work with them. Develop those deep internal relationships with your partners so they know what you do and how you would add value to their clients. Be sure to ask for some origination credit if you're helping bring in business proactively. After all, it also helps them to increase their bandwidth. If you're a solo, this can be done just as well with your existing strategic partners.

Farmer activity #1: One of the easiest ways to begin farming for new originations is to get active on social media. The cost and time needed to get started here are negligible.

If you're a big fan of the movie Shawshank Redemption, you know the line, "Get busy living or get busy dying." That's how I feel about social media and LinkedIn in particular. In case you were wondering, if you're not active on LinkedIn, you're the one dying. FYI, there's a killer tutorial on LinkedIn best practices on my YouTube channel if you look me up by name.

Farmer activity #2: Writing and publishing articles is another farming activity that will pay off over time if you're consistent in your efforts. The best part of article writing is the ability to repurpose the content for your monthly newsletter, email blast, social media and posting on your website/blog. I've even done an audio version of my article from last month to broaden the content even further. I'm writing this article on a Saturday morning, when clients aren't available to meet, so it's perfect.

Farmer activity #3: It's never been easier than now to create video content. You used to have to hire a videographer, schedule a day off to film and then it would take weeks to get anything finished. Today, you can develop amazing content on Zoom or with your smart phone. Just write down 5-10 things that you solve every day and create 30-second to two-minute clips on your subject matter. As long as the sound and visual are clean, people will watch and listen to you. Like with #2 above, this content can be repurposed in a variety of ways.

Now that we've redefined the hunter-farmer paradigm, you need to decide which you are, or a combination of the two. My feeling, as a born hunter, is that you should try to do both the hunting and the farming to ensure you get that book of business built right away. Smart lawyers plan, execute and follow through on their biz-dev efforts to ensure the best outcomes each year. If you want to BE THAT LAWYER, start hunting and/or farming today.

CHAPTER 26

SURVEY SAYS: TOP ISSUES ATTORNEYS ARE HAVING WITH BUSINESS DEVELOPMENT

In working with thousands of attorneys over the past 15-plus years, I always ask the same question, "With regards to business development, what are your primary challenges, frustrations and concerns?" My clients know I call these "CFCs." Since, apparently, I have little to do on a snowy weekend in Chicago, I've compiled my notes and slimmed down the list to the top five. Here they are in no particular order and how you might consider addressing them moving forward.

CFC #1. "I have no time to do business development and marketing."

It's not a coincidence that this issue comes first on the list. Only YOU have the ability to change your future for the better, and effectively managing your time is job number one! Failure to do so at your own career peril. The good news is that time management is a learned skill. Here are three things that might help get you on a better path:

- Read the books, "Getting Things Done" by David Allen and "Time Mastery" by Walt Hampton. Both offer invaluable tips and strategies for overcoming your time crisis.

- Track your day (in 15-minute increments) to identify your time weaknesses. Focus on isolating the jobs you're doing that should be delegated or outsourced. Many attorneys are doing $25-40 dollar an hour tasks, when they are billable well over $400 an hour.
- Learn to say the word, "No." If you're truly serious about building your own book of business, you can't continue to do everyone else's work. You'll need to free some time up in order to execute on your own business development initiatives.

CFC #2. "I have no idea how, or even where to get started."

Are you complaining that they never taught you this in law school? That might be the number one adage I hear daily. So, you're not alone, as until recently "sales" was never taught in any school. Again, business development is a learned skill that must be mastered to get to the finish line more quickly and with less effort. I personally know that there are three terrific books you would enjoy and get great value from reading, MINE! While this might sound like a shameless plug, I'm happy to email you free copies if you'd like. Otherwise go on Amazon and grab "Sales-Free Selling," "The Attorneys Networking Handbook" or "The Ambitious Attorney." For the more serious and determined attorneys, I have a variety of programs that would short-cut the learning to significantly grow your book this year. Happy to help.

CFC #3. "I'm not staying in front of my best connections for referrals."

Whether you are really well connected or you've worked diligently to grow an amazing network, it's possible that you are not fully engaging them. For many attorneys it's all about staying top of mind, so when something comes up you're the first call they make. Here are three simple ways to generate momentum to light up your inbox:

- Use LinkedIn for posting, commenting and sharing. You're already on LinkedIn, you might as well use it. Post two-to-three times a week to get your name in front of your top connections. It also doesn't hurt to like, comment and share your best connections' posts. Trust me, they're watching and anxious to see who's engaging with their content.

- Create a list of your top 10-20 connections to email or call once a month. Ask, "how can I help you, or be a stronger resource?" Maybe the email is to congratulate them on some personal or business accomplishment. Whatever the case, don't let these contacts get cold.

- Outsource an email campaign or newsletter to engage your audience and provide value. Even if you're at a mid-market or large law firm, it's still "You, Inc." Utilize your assistant or outsource a marketing person to execute on this for you once a month. It does make a difference in staying top of mind with 500-5000 contacts.

CFC #4. "I'm terrible at making the ask."

Boy oh boy, you're not alone here, my friend. This is a big one, and I totally get why. You're not in sales, you never wanted to be in sales and you hate being sold to–and so do your contacts. My answer is, then don't do it.

In my world, lawyers need to build trust, ask questions, actively listen and demonstrate empathy. If someone has a legal need and you follow those instructions, the prospective client will want to SELL YOU on why you should take them on as a client. While this might sound like common sense, it takes skill, practice and continual improvement to get to your desired results.

CFC #5. "I need to get in front of higher-level decision makers."

How do you get in front of General Counsels, CEOs and Directors of HR? For most successful rainmaking attorneys, it's all about having strong strategic partners. These are well connected professional who are trusted advisors to the decision makers, maybe like you are with your clients. The key here is to be strategic. Ask yourself, which lawyer, CPA, wealth advisor or consultant is dealing with the same decision makers I am? Consider the geography, title of the person you'd like to reach, size of business, specific industry, and other important factors to determine if the strategic partner is truly well aligned with you.

While I know these issues don't magically go away through wishing, hoping or complaining, they are all solvable with the right mindset, learned skills and intelligent effort. As a lawyer, you're all about solving problems and finding creative solutions. Maybe now is the best time to solve the biggest challenge of all: your success in business development.

PART 2: MARKETING

CHAPTER 27

FIND OUT IF SOCIAL MEDIA IS FOR YOU

As a marketing and business development coach, one of the most common questions I hear from attorneys is regarding the value of posting on social media.

Opinions vary on this subject to such a great extent that I thought I would create a social media test for you to better understand if it's a worthwhile endeavor.

It's important to be honest with yourself to ensure you make the right decisions with your time moving forward.

Social media assessment

Rate yourself on a scale of 1 to 5 (1 = not at all and 5 = definitely yes).

1. Do you have something of value to offer a given audience?

2. Do you enjoy writing and speaking?

3. Are you looking to grow your brand in the marketplace?

4. Are referrals important to your practice?

5. Do you understand the value of using social media?

Great, now score yourself. Here's the key to see if social media is really for you:

5 to 10 — You may have better things to do with your time. Perhaps focus on leveraging existing relationships and standard networking.

11 to 17 — With a little help and education, social media may be a good investment of time and effort.

18 to 25 — You're already on your way. Let's take this to the next level!

OK, now that you have your score, it's important to share the reasons I asked you these questions and how this may help you move forward to set social media aside for the time being.

Let's start with the first question. Do you have something of value to offer a given audience?

This is critical because social media for lawyers is primarily about education and updating your audience on the law and how it may impact them.

If you are not sure who your audience is or what you would even share with them, what would you even say on Twitter? As an attorney, you have to be an expert on your subject matter and speak intelligently on the subject in order to get value from using social media. Start there and then let's come back to discuss.

The second question relates to your enjoyment of speaking and writing on your practice area or industry. If you are not passionate about what you do, there's little chance that you're going to invest time speaking and writing on the subject. Some of the best social marketers are reading, writing and speaking on their subject, weekly, and it's impacting how they are viewed as an expert in the marketplace.

I would love our third point to include everyone, but let's be realistic with each other. Building your brand in the marketplace is hard work. What type of effort are you really making? Approximately 80 percent of attorneys are worker bees focusing only on the work. While doing great work helps to build your brand, it's not even close to where it could be.

Becoming recognized first as "the" person to call for a legal problem is the epitome of success as a practitioner. Social media may be the best way to accomplish this, outside of kicking butt in court or making your client happy.

The fourth question asked related to referrals and their importance to you and growing your practice.

This relates directly to the point made above, while also leveraging social media to get in front of new referral sources that don't know you but read your posts. Being regularly in front of your audience will lead to referrals from places and people you never expected to hear from.

The last point might be the most important of all. It's nearly impossible to get value from social media if you don't understand it's purpose and how to effectively use it.

There are so many moving parts, it can be confusing to anyone looking to leverage it effectively. LinkedIn, Facebook and Twitter are different platforms. To help with this, let's talk about the big three and the key focus points associated with each.

LinkedIn
The most used business-to-business social media platform. Most business professionals are now on this site, so let's

look at the key terminology as it related to posting and brand building.

The main way to get the word out on LinkedIn is through posting updates or an article. This is a great way to share wins, new laws and your business point of view on your subject-matter expertise. Since you can't say you're an expert, you might as well demonstrate it in your writing and posting of content.

Be sure to find and use a dynamic picture and headline with your posts. The best posts are the ones that get seen, read, liked and inspire comments. Become a stalker by following and reading the posts of other successful attorneys. This will provide ideas and proven methodologies that you can spin into your own unique posting style.

Facebook

While this social network might be better for consumer-focused attorneys, let's not abandon the value of using it. CEOs, GCs and various referral sources are all on Facebook daily.

Building followers and fans can lead to new business if you stay with it and post interesting and valuable content. Developing fan pages, for example, can allow you to communicate directly with your well-connected friends and clients alike. Like with LinkedIn, it's important to utilize images and video to engage your audience and get discussions going with your base.

Twitter

You're either a part of the conversation or you're not. Twitter allows you to have a voice in the marketplace that you can control. Are you going to share humorous observations or broadcast industry information that's educational or thoughtful?

While posting comments is helpful to get your brand out there, most experts agree that Twitter is best used to engage your clients and potential strategic partners in a dialogue. Again, you are controlling the conversation or, oblivious, that there's even one to be had?

As you can imagine, it's difficult to write on a subject and summarize it down to a Daily Law Bulletin article. My hope is that it helps you think more strategically about social media and whether you should be using it or not.

Don't get overwhelmed, as there are outlets to outsource social media if you want help or don't have time to get directly involved. Many lawyers and law firms outsource to companies like mine to help take the pressure off, but we still need direction and engagement from you to make it work.

Right now, content is king. This means that you're either visible and growing or hidden and shrinking. Think of the world and how it's changed in the past two years.

As an attorney, growing your brand and driving originations has never been more important. Based on your score, it might be time to get educated on social media to take it to the next level.

CHAPTER 28

E-MAIL MARKETING: CONSTANT AND STEADY

I am asked almost daily about the benefits of e-mail marketing and newsletters. While I'm a huge advocate of this type of marketing, it's not always a fit for every lawyer or law firm.

Typically, I ask a few questions that help identify if there's value in expending limited resources on this marketing endeavor.

• Do you have 100 or more people to keep in touch with?
• Do you have something new or important to communicate?
• Are you looking to keep your clients and develop new ones?

If the answer is yes to any one of these questions, then please keep reading. If the answer is no, it may be because you are just starting out, you're in a "worker bee" role at your firm or you are close to retirement and looking to slow things down.

For all those who answered affirmatively, here are the top five reasons an e-mail newsletter would be of great value to you in sustaining and growing your practice. Also, be sure to read the last paragraph if you're serious about executing on an effective e-mail campaign.

Stay top of mind

Having something to e-mail your clients, colleagues and friends each month to keep in touch is rarely a losing proposition. Think about it, how long does it take to e-mail 100 to 1,000 people each month? You and I both know you don't have time not to do that. An e-mail newsletter allows you to get your name and important content in front of your people, your clients, on a regular basis, where you alone cannot.

One of the main reasons attorneys lose clients today is lack of regular communication and face time. Statistically, it takes six times more energy, money and time to find a new client, than it does to keep the one you have.

Building brand equity

I wrote earlier about the importance of being a leader in your field and growing your brand equity. There's no reason why that can't be done through your monthly newsletter.

Here's an opportunity to take your finest ideas, strongest wins, insightful articles and best resources and share them with your clients, strategic partners and colleagues.

In addition to adding value to these existing relationships, you're demonstrating why they need you in their life. This is also where word of mouth is key. Your audience members forward your material to their audiences, who then do the same. It's amazing how people love to share great content that benefits others.

Promote what's new

Do you have a new logo? New area of focus? New white paper? New win in appellate court? People love new! It's exciting to read about positive changes that people are making in their business and personal lives. For example, let's say that you share a favorable decision in court. One of your past clients sees this and decides to call you for a similar matter she is dealing with. Now you may get a client back that's been dormant for years. Nice, right?

Better quality leads

What's the easiest way to find new business? Networking? Cold calling? Attending conferences? The answer is "no, no and no." As I mentioned, the best way to get new business is from your existing clients and strategic partnerships.

What e-mail marketing can offer you is prequalified business leads. Again, the people who already know you and know your work are the most likely to use you again and refer you to others. While I'm not suggesting that these other marketing efforts aren't worthwhile, statistically they are less likely to convert and take much longer to vet.

Generate more website traffic

The final point I'll make on e-mail marketing is the importance of driving traffic to your website. That being said, if your website is terrible and outdated, you can skip to the end of my article.

A bad or outdated website will typically turn away business, rather than generate it. For those who have successful and well thought out websites, it's of critical importance to get people there. This is where you house your blog, bio, testimonials and other relevant information that can convert your network into new or repeat business. Your e-mail newsletter can do just that, leading people down a path and getting that phone call you are looking for.

Now, you might be thinking, "What the #$@! do I know about setting up a newsletter, let alone how it works to drive business?" Well, there are two options you have for this. First, go online and research options for automation tools like Mail Chimp or Constant Contact.

They will provide many videos and articles on how to do this. But, if you are strapped for time and do not want to learn this, let alone execute on this, there are many companies that actively take this over for you.

Like your website, your newsletter is an extension of you and your brand. If you decide to outsource this service, be sure you meet with an expert who understands your business and practice and that you can trust to get this marketing piece done properly.

CHAPTER 29

LAW FIRM WEBSITES: BASIC BROCHURE OR BRANDING TOOL FOR SUCCESS?

Recently, I was reviewing a law firm's website with the managing partner to discuss his thoughts on the existing platform. He looked at his site and without hesitation said, "I think it's fine." This answer is not uncommon as websites from the 1990s and 2000s are used every day in the legal profession to share the most basic of information with whomever may stumble across it.

Unfortunately, this managing partner, like most, is totally lost on the value of a good website and how it acts as a culture shifter, business generator and brand builder for a law firm.

A simple way to understand whether it's time to update your website is to ask yourself the following questions. Just check answer "yes" or "no." Once completed, we can move on to discuss the real benefits of this seemingly scary and possibly daunting investment.

1. Does my website separate my firm from other law firms who sell similar services?
2. When my clients go to my website, is there relevant legal and business content to share with them?

3. Would my website attract a new (and younger) attorney to come work here?

4. Am I happy with the current culture of our firm? For instance, are we working in silos, afraid to share clients? Are we actively promoting our diversity? Are we actively promoting our goodwill and public interest?

5. Does our website deliver high-level prospective clients with more work (not to mention more from your existing clients)?

If you answered "no" to most of these questions, this should be a wake-up call for you to consider investing in fixing these troubled areas. To help educate you on this complicated subject and to ensure you don't overspend, I'm going to answer these questions for you now.

1. Does my website separate my firm from other law firms who sell similar services?

The book "Blue Ocean Strategy" by W. Chan Kim and Renee Mauborgne states that the sea is bloody red with competition and that the key to sustainable success to find the open blue waters.

A unique and well-designed website can do that for you. Let's say you are competing for a new litigation matter and the prospective client views your old worn-out website versus a creative content-rich site. All other things being even, which would they choose to handle their complicated matter?

While this might not have been important 10 years ago, today it's of critical importance. It's how people make informed decisions. Would you go to a restaurant that had images online that were severely outdated and appeared dirty?

2. *When my clients go to my website, is there relevant content to share with them?*

In business, cash is king. In marketing, content is king! This is the new reality that we all live in. Having up-to-date, expertly written content is more critical than ever to growing your brand and driving traffic to your business.

Having your own blog on your site, for example, can be a game-changer in your space. Not only will you be better known as a serious player, it will help drive clients and new prospective clients to your website — and to you!

Think about it this way — your website is face-to-face with your audience at moments when you are not. A well-designed website allows you to have 24/7 control of both your messages and your audience's perception of you. In sum, the website is working even when you're not.

3. *What does my website say about the firm that would attract a new attorney to come work here?*

Picture this. You are paying a recruiter 20 percent to find you a qualified attorney with $500,000 in portable business. This attorney would be an incredible catch for your firm. She interviews and is considering two other firms in addition to yours. Is it possible that when she researches your firm and sees an old-fashioned website that lacks diversity, she may go a different direction? Of course! You may not even realize that this is happening.

The 30- and 40-year-olds are the future of your business, and they are hyper-focused and critical on websites that are old and outdated. Your website can be the best recruiting tool for your firm when done properly. One good and profitable hire could literally pay for your site for years to come.

4. Am I happy with the current culture of our firm? Are we working in silos, afraid to share clients? Are we actively promoting our diversity? Are we actively promoting our goodwill and public interest?

Just like your clothes reflect your style, websites reflect the expertise and culture of your firm. Sometimes we need to reinvest in how we look to stay relevant with the times. Improving your website won't necessarily fix a bad culture, but it could.

The key here is that the fish may stink from the head down. This means that your top players need to be the drivers behind a fresh and new marketing initiative.

Without this support, the investment may not be fully utilized to grow business moving forward. If you can get the team behind a new look and approach to marketing and business development, it will help to improve productivity and positivity in the office.

5. Does our website deliver high-level prospective clients with more work (not to mention more from your existing clients)?

OK, here's the big misnomer. "I don't want business leads from the internet. They are not going to pay our fees." While it may be true that some legal verticals are better for lead generation online than others, you may be looking at websites with the wrong mindset. Getting to the top of Google is only one element to driving new business.

The better way to think about it is to consider your past and existing clients as well as past and existing prospective clients. A good website, blog, newsletter and tasteful advertising can go a long way to driving business back to you again and again.

Having an interactive website and marketing program will target the clients that you want, more so than the small deals that may not be worth your time.

The reality is that most law firms have outdated and ineffective websites that really get nothing accomplished for you and your firm.

It's no surprise that you may find little value in this type of investment. Look, you don't have salespeople out there for you, so maybe having a classy and effective 24/7 sales tool might be a good idea.

I hope this was helpful and that you now understand that this is not an expense, but rather a valuable investment for the future of your firm.

CHAPTER 30

LAW FIRM MARKETING: 5 THINGS YOU MAY NOT KNOW

While there are many different things you should be doing to market your law firm this year, there are a few "must do's" that can mean the difference between simply surviving or really thriving with your marketing efforts.

The first step is identifying your target clients, followed by utilizing one or more of these points to drive the business through your doors. The most important marketing step that is skipped by attorneys relates directly to strategy, or more often, lack thereof.

Most marketing decisions are made on the fly like a trauma center or ER. You might be hustling to get a press release out today or update your website tomorrow. It's like applying a Band- Aid to a gaping wound. The solution for this is to run a complete audit on your marketplace and your overall marketing campaigns. Three things you could do right away include:

Look at your past and existing client base to understand the "who, what, when, where, how and why" that makes up your yearly business. You may be able to identify where the opportunities in the marketplace will be in the future. This information will also help you make better decisions for investing your marketing time and dollars.

Review your website's analytics. This is the back end of your website that shows you where all your visitors are coming from, what they are looking for on your website and if they are actually taking action toward contacting you. If your current website or marketing provider isn't reviewing this data with you monthly, they may not really be helping you with your marketing at all.

Track all of your past marketing to see what's been paid back, versus what was tried and wasted. Investing in sponsorships or local advertising might have been money well spent, or it may have been a swing and a miss. Either way, you have the opportunity through tracking to make better decisions in the future.

The second marketing tip I'd like to suggest relates specifically to your website. The three greatest mistakes attorneys make here include:

- Lack of understanding your prospective client's mindset and what motivates them to contact you.
- No clear strategy for your website to drive your brand up in the marketplace.
- A website created on a shoestring budget and hope that it's "good enough."

The solution for these issues is not a one-size-fits-all. Most solo and small law firms don't possess the time, education or strategic foresight to create a website that truly illustrates their professionalism, success and unique business proposition. Websites and website marketing for lawyers changes frequently, just like the law is constantly changing. Find a strategic marketing leader internally or externally to ensure your marketing is done right and updated often.

The third element you need to know relates to content. In the world of business, cash is king. In the world of marketing, content reigns supreme. Your brand, website and social media all rely on content to ensure that you stay relevant and findable in the marketplace. Failure to produce quality content may leave you behind when things get tough or as more competition moves into the already busy space you are in. It's important to note that Google is always changing its algorithms, so you must adapt with them. Here are some important points to consider:

• Be sure that the subject you are writing on contains the key words that people are actually searching for online to find you or the area of law you are writing about. There's a reason why this column's title on the web is "Law firm marketing: Five key elements you may not know about." See? It's right there for Google to enjoy!

• Provide high-quality exhaustive content that takes traditional blogging to another level. We recommend 1,200 to 2,500 words to ensure Google sees you as the expert on the subject you are writing on.

• Do everything possible to get your writing onto reputable and relevant websites that link back to your website. Google wants to provide valuable guidance to their users based on what they are searching for. The back links you get from highly regarded websites will do this for you.

The fourth key element relates directly to how you connect and stay top-of-mind with your network. The two key drivers are social media and email campaigns. You are either out there adding value to your network of friends, colleagues, strategic partnerships and clients, or you're falling behind the thousands of other attorneys who are working tirelessly to capture their attention away from you. A few things to consider here might be:

• If you spend any real time on social media, you see the same people over and over again. If asked, you could point out three people you regularly see on Facebook or LinkedIn. If these individuals are positive and providing good content, you might consider them for a referral if one came up. They are much more likely to be thought of than someone who doesn't exist in this realm at all.

• Set up a newsletter for your network to stay in front of them. The content I mentioned above would be ideal to educate your clients while also staying in front of them on a regular basis. If you already have a newsletter, I'd recommend reviewing the data to understand who is opening it up and what they might be clicking. This information is typically ignored, which is a mistake. You may identify clients or contacts that you can proactively reach out to in order to get them in the door or provide additional content or value to them.

The fifth and final point I'll make is regarding your overall marketing execution. Marketing is not something that's one and done. It must be a consistent part of your law practice business plan to see real results over time. So, the next thing you'll say is, "How does one possibly find the time to do all of this?" Here are three suggestions that might help:

• Learn it! You don't need to know everything to improve your marketing. You can read books, watch videos or get trained on two or three elements that will help you grow your practice. Just prioritize what you want to learn and schedule time to do it.

• Delegate it! Some office managers, paralegals and younger associates have experience and skills at writing or social media. You may be able to get them trained up to help with execution. That being said, you may still have to outsource the strategy part and legal writing to ensure success.

• Outsource it! I am not a lawyer, and you are not a marketing professional, so hand over the reins. As long as you work together with a solid marketing professional in a collaborative way, good results should happen. As I mentioned earlier, be sure there's a strong focus on strategy before execution.

As the legal landscape continues to become more challenging, you must recognize that business will not always be coming your way. Preparation for the future means being open minded to new ideas and investing your time, money and energy accordingly. Remember that you're in the "business of law," so it's important to treat your marketing as a part of the overall business spend. Most businesses set aside 5-15% of their yearly revenue for marketing and business development. In case you are bad with math, the average should be $10,000 a year for every $100,000 you collect that year.

CHAPTER 31

BUILDING BRAND EQUITY REQUIRES THOUGHT AND SIMPLE, BUT IMPORTANT, STEPS

One of the areas attorneys struggle with is building their personal brand equity in the marketplace.

I define personal brand equity, or PBE, as "the value premium that an attorney generates from their perception in the marketplace."

The question you may need to ask yourself is, "What is the current perception of me or my practice in the legal marketplace?" Is it positive, negative or nonexistent? Whatever the case, here are five solid ways that will help you build, repair or grow your current brand in whatever marketplace or practice area you're in.

PBE No. 1 — Google yourself and take action now!
If you're like me, you've Googled yourself at some point. Today, it's more important than ever to do this as potential buyers and referral sources are using Google as a direct resource of information to learn about you.

There may be negative comments or ratings that you're unaware of. In addition, you may find that there's nothing about you, which means you don't exist (to buyers of legal services). On the other hand, type in the name of an attorney whose name you hear regularly. There may be five to 10 pages of search results that clearly demonstrate how this attorney has built his or her PBE.

It has never been more important to make sure your blog post, court wins, published articles and events are all available for the world to see. Failure to load these branding moments into your website or blog are missed opportunities you can't easily get back.

PBE No. 2— Go grassroots: It's time to network.

While it's of critical importance to build your online presence, don't forget to shake hands and kiss some babies along the way. I can't think of too many highly branded rainmaker attorneys that have skipped this step.

Take an hour and research events, conferences and groups that will allow you to meet prospective clients and high-level referral sources. But that's not all! Once you've met them, you need to grab a coffee or lunch, too, on a one-on-one level. Building rapport and finding synergies to refer and work together is a major component of successful brand building.

Try to set a goal for yourself to meet a few solid players each month that will enjoy spreading your name around and talking you up. Think about your favorite restaurant, store or medical practitioner; you probably go out of your way to tell people about how happy you are with them. It's even possible no one has asked you! Just remember, no one wins the race by sitting at a desk.

PBE No. 3 — Seriously, that's your website!

Why do you dress up for work each day? Why not just show up in flip-flops and a tank top? That's exactly what people think about you when they see your terribly outdated and poorly constructed website. Maybe it used to be an afterthought, but today it's critical to how you're viewed in the marketplace. Don't think for a minute that buyers of legal services aren't reviewing your website or bio before calling — or maybe not calling.

It doesn't have to cost a fortune to redo or update your current platform. Holding off on this one investment may be costing you money as potential clients exit the site to move on to other possible options.

The three main reasons people leave your website are website speed, lack of quality information and poor "calls to action." It's important to recognize that it's not about how you use a website, rather it's how your prospective clients, existing clients and potential laterals do.

PBE No. 4 — Get connected, stay connected and add value whenever possible.

You might agree that competition and price pressures in the legal space have never been more severe. My father practiced in the 1980s and 1990s and never had to worry about these things, whereas you should be losing a little sleep over it. That being said, there are so many ways to connect and add value for people in your network, you just have to pay attention and take action.

Three things to focus on are your blog, creating social media posts and maintaining a strong newsletter. These "touch points" can be critical to maintaining your existing base of contacts, clients and potential clients well into the future.

For example, a well-executed post on LinkedIn or Facebook can trigger likes, shares and positive comment that elevate your PBE. The key is to stay top of mind with your network and within the marketplace as a whole. Being visible and providing quality content will prove to be worth its weight in gold as the referrals and repeat business continue to stream in.

PBE No. 5 — The wild card is ... niche!
While this is a subject I've written on before (see the previous chapter), it needs to be summarized here. When the market thinks about the best criminal attorney, aviation attorney or Securities and Exchange Commission attorney, who comes to mind? I'm sure you can name at least one in each area. The reason is because they've won more cases, written more about their area or spoken on their subject more than anyone else.

While the time might not be right for you to have such a definitive focus, it's something worth working toward. It may be hard to believe, but it took me about five years working with attorneys to decide to specialize in the legal profession.

Before that, I had experience working in more than 40 different industries. The key for me was identifying needs in a marketplace that weren't being fulfilled properly. The key before taking the plunge was to gain knowledge and experience while also identifying the opportunity for growth. Once lawyers and law firms became more than 50 percent of my business, it became very clear to me that specialization made sense.

Take the time to review your client base, industries and professions served and what the trends are to determine if it's time to really focus on one thing. Once you've decided your niche, review points one to four above and take aggressive action to build your PBE.

As you continue your journey as an attorney, remember that you don't have to do this alone. There are resources for everything today from software to administrative help to marketing experts (like me!) that can take the nonlegal work off your hands. It may be the best investment you can make in your future as things continue to become more challenging.

CHAPTER 32

HOW TO DRAW MEDIA ATTENTION TO YOUR STORY TIME AND AGAIN

While effective business development is a surefire way to increase your book from year to year, it's important to remember that marketing and public relations can dramatically accelerate your business development efforts.

If you think about a skyscraper rising up to the sky, you must also look down to the base that holds up the behemoth. Taking 15 to 30 minutes a week to focus on growing your brand in the marketplace through positive PR could be an incredibly rewarding endeavor.

"But how do I do that?" you may ask. Well, continue reading Fretzin's five ways to get noticed by the media and you'll find out. Here we go!

Step 1: Control your own story.
You either own your own website, your own LinkedIn profile or your own blog. One way or another you have the ability to write unique and forward-thinking articles to demonstrate your expertise.

While this does take time, you may be practicing for 40-plus years and you will need contact for all those years. The earlier you begin to write or speak, the easier it will be to approach the media or, even better, get singled out and called by them.

Be sure to have a professional-looking presence on anything you do on the web. This will be the first thing any journalist will see before reaching out to you. If you think your website or social media pages look unprofessional or out-of-date, they will think so, too.

One way to find out how you come across is to simply search for yourself online. If things look incomplete, unprofessional and you only have a few search results under your name, you may have some work to do before following the next four steps.

Step 2: Write content that is relevant for today and into the future.

The idea here is to be a "mover and shaker" in your practice area or industry to ensure you get noticed. Be the first one with the story or exclusive to be relevant to the journalist's audience. They want it first, fast and exclusive.

Do your research before writing or speaking to demonstrate that you are a thought leader in your space.

For example, if you're in the estate planning and tax space, you need to study the news and get ongoing feedback regarding the impact of any new tax laws on various business entities or the economy.

Maybe you have a specific twist for small business owners and you can drive that angle to a particular media outlet like Entrepreneur, Inc. magazine or the entrepreneurs' section of The New York Times.

If your story has interesting data points or you see a trend, it could be gold to the journalists you're targeting. Which takes us to our next step.

Step 3: Target your best media contacts.
Journalists today are looking for content — always! There may be a serious win-win outcome when you take the time to introduce yourself and share a new story. Here are a few ways to accomplish this simple task:

• Research on Google or LinkedIn the journalists who have written articles in your city, practice area or industry. It never hurts to follow them on social media and like or comment on their blog posts and articles. Flattery, done with sincerity, doesn't hurt.

• Send an e-mail to introduce yourself. Be sure to provide a link to your website or LinkedIn page and let them know you like their writing. Try referencing a specific article that he or she wrote that hit home for you.

• Provide your best story on a cutting-edge or relevant topic and let the writer know there's more where that came from.

• Be sure to provide your contact information and thank them in advance for their time.

• If you don't hear back, reach out one to two more times with new and interesting stories to see if he or she might bite on something over time.

Step 4: Write news releases to get noticed.
Another way to get found and raise your identity in the marketplace is to begin writing news releases around new laws, trends or legal battles won. This is rarely done by solos and small firm attorneys but needs to be explored in order

to rise to the top. Today there are news release websites that will, for a reasonable investment, blast your story out to hundreds of media outlets.

Step 5: Don't lose touch or your momentum.
Once you've been discovered by a journalist, the most important next step is to simply have one! Go ahead and connect with your new friend on social media so he or she can stay up to speed on you and your posts. Also, be sure to provide exclusives to your journalist so she feels a sense of partnership.

This will help when it's time to reciprocate on a new article and he or she needs a few quotes.

It might even make sense to create a list of journalists and work to communicate on a monthly or quarterly basis. Staying top of mind is half the battle with journalists these days.

I know this may sound a bit daunting, which is why you need to be organized. What can you delegate to your staff and what can only be done by you? Conducting research and executing a written piece or a speaking engagement can be demanding on your time. Focus on topics that will get you noticed and that the media will find interesting to ensure your time is well spent.

CHAPTER 33

SOCIAL MEDIA FOR LAWYERS: DEVELOPING YOUR PERSONAL BRAND TO DRIVE NEW BUSINESS

One of the most common questions I'm asked as a business development coach for attorneys is, "Should I be posting on social media and is this a good use of my time and energy?"

You'll love my answer. It depends. The first thing you need to ask yourself is, "What am I trying to accomplish in my career?" "Who am I trying to target?" and "Am I willing to take time away from other things to get there?" If the answer is the affirmative, you may want to consider getting in the game or stepping up your current lackluster performance. Here are three simple steps to get started or bring your game to the next level in 30 days or less.

Step #1. Answer the questions I asked at the beginning of this piece; what are you trying to accomplish and who are you targeting as your audience? Assuming growth is desired, you must consider your targets and if social media is a relevant way to attract them.

From my experience there are two key targets that you may want to focus on. The first group is direct prospective clients, including general counsels, CEOs, and all forms of executives who can hire you directly. The second is strategic partners, or referral sources who may send the first group of targets your way. If one or both of these groups are engaged on social media, you may have some success if you have the right connections, content and social interactions.

Do yourself a favor before going any further by creating a list of these two targeted groups. Try writing down the names of five prospects and five known referral sources. Then look on LinkedIn to see if you can find them with "active" profiles. By active, I mean that they have photos, summaries, active email addresses, over 250 connections and have history of engaging in the platform (LinkedIn in this example). If you're seeing a positive trend from the names you're researching, LinkedIn may be a good place to start.

Step #2. Create a social media calendar to ensure that your posts include quality, consistency and are focused in the following areas:

- Education – Write or repost content that is valuable and interesting to your audience. This is an opportunity to get more value from the content you've researched or created. For example, I write this column for the Chicago Daily Law Bulletin every month. Then I post it on LinkedIn and Facebook to get more traction then CDLB alone. My posts get seen by the over 9,000 connections I have on LinkedIn.

- Rant – Take a stand on something you feel strongly about. This can define and differentiate you from the other attorneys who are only playing it safe. Here's an opportunity for you to demonstrate authenticity, which is what connects people to you in a meaningful way. No need for images or name dropping here. Just dig in and have some fun with this (up to 1300 characters). You'll be amazed at the traction you can create.

- Query – Ask a question that may generate comments and dialogue with your targeted audience (no politics or religion). LinkedIn even has a new polling feature that allows you to formalize a Q & A to your specifications.

o Appreciation – Post other people's content and share your gratitude for them and how they help others. Be sure to @name the person or people with whom you are giving praise.

In addition to these types of posts, be sure to commit to a certain number of posts per week. Only with consistent effort can your brand be built on social media. Consider that you may need to post two-to-five times a week for six months to get things on the right track. Also, consider bringing your assistant into the mix or hiring a social media assistant to help you and ensure this gets done every week.

Step #3. It's called "social" media for a reason. Posting content alone isn't going to get you to the promised land. It is imperative that you like, comment and share posts with your community to engage them in a positive way. This can be a time suck, so you may want to build out your list of targeted strategic partners, clients and prospects to ensure you focus on them versus the general public.

For example, I regularly comment and add my two cents with many of my strategic partners in the legal space. Many lawyers like to talk shop around marketing and business development. I love kicking in my ideas and experiences to add value to their posts. I often find other users liking and commenting on my comments. GOAL! We have engagement.

While there are so many elements of social media that we hate or even despise, there are just as many silver linings if we look in the right places. For myself and many of my attorney clients, we focus on LinkedIn as it's more professional and business focused. One thing to remember, you are either a part of the conversation or you're not. When it comes to brand building as a lawyer through social media, you need to decide if you are in or out. If it's not for you, that's okay. There are many other ways to build your brand without engaging on social media. That being said, effectively utilizing these platforms will shorten the process of becoming well known and a leader in your space.

CHAPTER 34

PODCASTING FOR LAWYERS: FOR A SELECT FEW, IT MAY BE THE PROMISED LAND

Have you ever watched a late-night talk show and wondered, could I do that? I have. That being said, it was never something I took seriously or pursued beyond my creative and wandering mind. Interestingly enough, today we are all "out there" on social media asking questions, sharing our thoughts and providing strong opinions. In some ways, we are all doing our own version of "MeTV."

While podcasting might have been around for 20-plus years, most people began listing when our phones provided accessibility through our apps. Personally, I've only been listening to podcasts for about five years. I love the way the information and entertainment are delivered, along with a wide variety of show options. Most importantly for me, it's the ability to do other things while listening (e.g., walking the dog, driving or finally cleaning the garage) that is most compelling.

A few years ago I was invited to speak on my friend Tina Martini's show, Paradigm Shift (shout out to Tina!) about legal business development for lawyers. We had a blast and I had to inquire about her show to better understand what was really involved. She shared her experiences with me and I was intrigued by the potential to widen my audience and help more lawyers through quality content.

If you haven't already heard my show BE THAT LAWYER, it's worth a listen. We're currently producing two shows a week, with amazing guests who provide tactical and actionable ways to grow your law practice. The result after a year of doing podcasts has been nothing short of a "game-changer" for me. For the purposes of this article and to benefit you directly, here are five reasons you may want to start your own podcast.

Reason #1. Meet AMAZING new people. Part of running an interview-style show is obtaining and speaking with interesting guests. In addition to targeting specific people who might be a good fit, it's remarkable to see the guests who are being directed to you through your network, past guests and even public relations folks looking to get their clients on air. You can really grow your network of influencers by inviting quality people on your show.

Reason #2. Don't say you're an expert, prove it! There's something magical that happens in an interview when you're actively listing and present; you have the ability to share wisdom with your audience in a truly authentic way. While it's generally a conversation between two people, the questions you ask during the back-and-forth repartee and the idea-sharing that occurs can lead your listener to believe in your expertise. The end result may be a loyal following of listeners who want to engage with you.

Reason #3. You're creating amazing new content that can be easily repurposed. So you may be thinking, podcasting sounds like a lot of work and time that I don't have. If you're smart, you can outsource 90% of the production and focus solely on the guest interviews. Once a show is completed, you can upload it and let your production team do the rest. Then, you can have it transcribed and edited for a blog, you can create a YouTube video around it, or post it on your website to help with SEO (Search Engine Optimization).

Reason #4. You may not get famous, but you will be noticed. There's something about podcasting that's different from all other forms of media. There's a cross-promotional element between you and your guest that acts as a branding multiplier. For example, when I post my podcast episode on LinkedIn and my guest does the same, we double our branding efforts with that combined effort. I get into their world and he/she gets into mine. Then on top of that, the audience may share the episode with others as well. The end result may be a boom in your branding efforts unlike anything you've seen before.

Reason #5. Hate doing business development? Let it come to you. Probably the best part of producing a quality podcast is the traction it creates for your business development efforts. When you get six months into it and start building a following, people really feel like they know you. Think about that. If trust is paramount to hiring a lawyer, you are building that through your honesty and authenticity. Additionally, you may interview GCs, CEOs and other high-profile people that might want to talk shop after the recording has stopped. What a wonderful way to get new business!

To be clear, starting your own podcast isn't for everyone. It takes creativity and an ongoing commitment to producing quality content that builds an audience. If you are interested in building your brand in a new and exciting way, podcasting may be the platform for you.

PART 3:

Networking

CHAPTER 35

LAW STUDENTS, NETWORKING IS NOW VITAL

I have had the great pleasure of speaking at a Chicago Bar Association event for young attorneys on the topic of networking.

After about 20 minutes, I observed how ravenously everyone was taking notes and the deep level of attentiveness that I was receiving from the participants. While this is not unique to me as a speaker in the legal space, there was something different in the eyes of audience. Fear.

Once the program concluded, I stuck around to chat with the attendees to better understand their mindset. A few of the comments were, "I have no idea how to network and am just trying to put myself out there."

And, "They never taught me any of this in law school." One first-year lawyer even remembered an adjunct professor saying, "If you're not networking, you're not working." The same lawyer then thanked me for my presentation where I explained and demonstrated different ways to actually do it.

Over the past 10 years, I have spoken at a number of young attorney events, but the fear and confusion on this day was palpable. For more than 200 years, law schools have focused on teaching the law to produce scholarly advocates to protect the rights of his or her clients.

There was never a need to teach networking or how to run a solo practice because lawyers were employed at firms where the primary focus was gaining experience as a lawyer. There was also an abundance of opportunities to get a job.

In economics, we all learned about supply and demand. In the case of the legal space today, the supply of lawyers is overtaking the demand. Especially in the case of the new grads and younger lawyers. With the legal landscape changing, it would only make sense that the law schools must change as well.

One attorney I interviewed was even involved in a 2014 report by the Illinois State Bar Association that revealed that law schools really aren't preparing their students for the challenging legal marketplace that currently exists.

Fortunately, I did uncover that there are some adjunct professors and career services professionals that discuss networking with their students, but it's just not enough. Networking is a learned skill that involves planning and processes to gain traction and ensure positive results.

These skills can be used for the job search, deciding to go solo or as an ongoing activity to grow a book of business. Even the simple skill of asking questions and listening to someone's answers will be critical to a lawyer's ongoing success and sustainability.

Over the past few months, I have been speaking with law schools to discuss this curriculum and its importance to the future of the legal profession. As I continue to develop content and drive these programs forward, here are three core elements that will be included:

Learning how to write a plan

All law school students need to learn how to develop a written plan for finding a job or going out on their own. They say, "Failing to plan is a plan to fail." It is imperative that students learn how to develop and write a plan to better prepare for any eventuality. If the job market were tight, it would be helpful to have developed inside connections to find a good firm or company to work for.

If there were struggles to find the right job, then developing a plan to partner with other solos to develop some business would be valuable.

Whatever the situation, one's ability to develop a plan will be the breakthrough moment for someone wanting a career in the legal space.

Learning how to really use social media

In the age of anytime information and promotion, anyone can use social media to improve their ability to find a job or increase exposure in the marketplace. LinkedIn, for example, allows its users to connect on the site and find inside connections that normally would be hidden.

For example, if we were friends and connected on LinkedIn, you could search through my connections to see the wide variety of general counsels and hiring lawyers that I know.

Asking me for an inside channel into these contacts is infinitely more effective than sending out cold resumes to job postings or firms you are interested in.

Learning the basics of communication, networking

As someone who has killed hundreds of hours by networking inefficiently, I can attest to the importance of structure and processes to follow when networking. These methodologies can be found through books, firm mentors or teachers like myself. For many attorneys, back in school this would be important, because it's not about whom you know anymore but rather how you leverage the relationships with those you know.

Failure to properly give and receive value in a structured way within your network can lead to countless unproductive hours at events and coffee meetings. While it's true that relationships take time, how much time and with whom you invest is in question.

Whether you are currently enrolled in law school, a recent grad or someone who is billing 2,000 hours a year for someone else's clients at your firm, learning to plan and execute on your networking has never been more important.

I know that the law schools today are aware of the need for networking classes, but they just haven't fully committed to the idea. My hope is that with further awareness and forward-thinking deans, graduates will be better equipped to acquire the jobs they are looking for.

CHAPTER 36

GET THE MOST OUT OF YOUR NETWORKING; TAKE THIS TEST AND GRADE YOURSELF

If you've read my book "The Attorney's Networking Handbook," you probably know that I am a big fan of effective networking. I use the word "effective" because networking done improperly is just a huge waste of time.

There are so many elements to networking that we can't possibly cover them in one column, so I thought it would make sense to have you take my survey to better identify where your strengths and weaknesses are, so that you can work to improve upon them.

Take 60 seconds to rate yourself on a scale of 1 to 5 (5 is always) and then we will review ways to improve each focus area. Enjoy!

Question No. 1: When at a networking event, do you focus 100 percent on the person who is speaking with you?

Question No. 2: When at a networking event, do you ask questions to identify how you can help someone else?

Question No. 3: When at a coffee meeting, do you identify one or two ways you can help or add value for the other person?

Question No. 4: During a one- on-one coffee meeting, do you help the other person identify contacts that would be beneficial to you, versus shying away from this task?

Question No. 5: After your first successful meeting, do you regularly follow up with your best contacts to keep the momentum going?

OK, now rate yourself and total up your score.

If your total was 5 to 10, you have a lot of work ahead to improve your effectiveness.

If your total was 11 to 17, you have minor adjustments to make.

If your total was 18 to 25, you are doing terrific, but there are always new things to learn, so don't get overconfident.

To get you started on the right path, here is one solution to each issue:

Suggestion No. 1: When at a networking event, focus 100 percent on the person who is speaking with you.
Don't push your card at them and stop worrying about impressing people with your canned fancy infomercial.

Instead, ask a few relationship-building business questions to get your new friend talking. For example, if she's an accountant, how about asking, "What do you enjoy about accounting?" or, "How did you get into that line of work?" I'm sure there a story behind their career and discussing it is a great way to build rapport.

Suggestion No. 2: When at a networking event, ask questions to identify how you can help someone else.

Once you've built the rapport as suggested above, ask, "What should I be listening for in a good referral for you?" There are two amazing elements to this question. First, you are being thoughtful to them and possibly helping them in their business development efforts.

Second, you are not committing to providing referrals to this person — yet. Asking isn't offering, which is important because you've only just met this person and shouldn't be providing referrals yet anyway. It may be too soon.

Suggestion No. 3: When at a coffee meeting, you identify one or two ways you can help or add value for the other person.
Now that you know this person better, you want to demonstrate that you have something to offer. If you're listening intently to your new friend, she should be cluing you in on whom she is looking to meet. Take some notes and identify someone worthwhile for her.

Suggestion No. 4: You help the other person identify people that would be beneficial to you, versus shying away from this task.
This is the one step that good networkers forget. They make referrals, which is terrific, but forget that people need to be led or coached to help you. Take the lead and help her to help you.

Work cooperatively to identify one or two good referrals that would work for you. In addition to walking away from the meeting with some traction, you are also able to test out your new friend to see if her follow-up skills are up to snuff. A win-win!

Suggestion No. 5: You regularly follow up with your best contacts to keep the momentum going after the first meeting was successful.

Another major mistake good networkers make is not staying tightly aligned with the referral partners who you've had success with in the past. It's either a hit-and-run, where you've gotten something and moved on, or you're just busy and forgot that this person has value to you and your business building efforts.

Make a list of your best strategic partners and follow up with them monthly to ensure they stay with you long-term.

The reality is that without some process, thought and methodology behind networking, it can be an unbillable nightmare for any attorney.

The next time you're out networking, try to follow a few of my guidelines and you'll see the improvements in your skills.

CHAPTER 37

NETWORKING TIPS TO BOOST ORIGINATIONS

As you're building or rewriting your business development plan for a new year, it might make sense to look at where improvements and efficiencies can be made. One critical area that's typically overlooked is networking. Any networking event you attend or coffee meeting you conduct can sap away your time at lightning speed. Here are my top five tips for any attorney looking to hit the mark in a new year on the networking front. Enjoy!

Tip 1: Go where the action is. While there are literally hundreds of events you can attend each month, it's of critical importance to focus on going where your best connections will be. Think about the people who need your services and where they might be. Then think about the people who also provide services to those end users and where they might be. That's the place to go.

For example, if you are a commercial litigator, your end clients might be general counsels or CEOs. Where are they when out of the office? Also, what other service providers sell to those general counsels and CEOs? How about middle market CPAs or e-Discovery consultants?

If you keep the end in mind when deciding what events to attend, you may improve your results.

Tip 2: Try talking less, asking more. While it is important to have an infomercial or elevator pitch ready to go, it's even more important to prepare yourself with questions for the people you meet at these events.

The goal is always to get someone else engaged in a conversation where you can learn about her, what she does for a living and find common ground.

I would recommend starting with the easy questions and drive to the more involved. Here are a few questions to choose from:

• "Is this your first time to this event?"

• "This is my first time here, what do you like about this group (or event)?"

• "What type of business are you in?"

• "Do you live in the city or the burbs?"

• "When you're not busy working, what do you do for fun?"

• "What do you enjoy most about your business (career)?"

• "What types of challenges are you seeing in your industry?"

• "What types of people are you most interested in meeting?"

• "What should I be listening for in a good referral for you?"

Tip 3: Three words: qualify, qualify, qualify. One of the biggest mistakes networkers make is not adequately qualifying the people they meet as it relates to next steps. As an attorney, your time is literally money; so don't agree to meet with everyone you meet.

If someone is a potential client for you, a potential referral partner for you or someone very well connected, there is a direct reason to meet. All other meetings should be taken with great skepticism.

Of course there are exceptions, but choose wisely. This may include "paying it forward" with younger people who you can help with finding a job or launching a new business. Otherwise, you will find that you have just wasted an hour or two with a "nice person" or an annoying salesman who will steal time right away from you.

Tip 4: When you do meet people for coffee, it's best to be prepared. LinkedIn, Facebook and Google are all available at your fingertips; you must use these tools to get prepared to meet someone new. It is simply unacceptable these days to merely show up and say, "So, tell me what do you do?"

Have your talking points and questions ready to go in order to make a good impression. This will ensure that you take the meeting in a positive direction from the get-go.

Tip 5: Always have next steps when it makes sense. Far too often meetings end with the usual, "Great meeting with you. Let's keep our eyes open for one another moving forward." It might be a love fest, but it's not good business acumen for growing originations.

Think about it this way. You meet with a doctor and see that he can make you feel better. Would you leave the next step open or flexible? Of course not! You'd get an appointment to visit again to cure the ailment.

When finishing up a networking meeting when energy is being generated, do your best to set up next steps with your new friend. This could be another meeting, inviting her to a networking group where you belong or inviting her to sit on a panel that you're organizing.

Whatever the case, don't leave a positive meeting without a specific next step forward. Just this one point will dramatically improve your chances of success when networking.

One of my favorite mantras is "There is no failure, only learning." This is so true in networking to ensure you aren't making the same mistakes year after year.

Try to implement at least one of these tips in the new year and you'll see the benefits materialize right before your eyes.

CHAPTER 38

HOW TO PICK UP SOME ACTUAL WORK FROM WORKING A CONFERENCE

When conference season is upon you, it's time to take stock of how you've benefited from these engagements.

As you may already know, these events can be time-consuming and expensive, netting little to no actual new business. Considering all those factors, it seems to defy logic that anyone still goes other than to obtain Continuing Legal Education credit.

Albert Einstein is well known for his definition of insanity, "Doing the same thing over and over and expecting a different result." Is that true for you as it relates to the way you work or don't work a conference?

The real value in attending conferences occurs when its participant is well prepared. Devising a plan that includes being added to the agenda as a presenter, obtaining an attendee list in advance and making a point of scheduling coffee meetings with prospective decision-makers prior to the conference's start are a few of the insider tips you must focus on.

With a well-thought-out plan, proper execution and prompt follow through, you can change the lackluster conference experiences in your past into results-oriented time where you actually generate new business.

To make my point crystal clear, think about it this way: Would you willingly head into a courtroom for trial without preparing first? Of course not. Just as there are tried-and-true trial preparation tactics you learned in school and on the job, there are some key "success elements" to obtaining new business from attending professional conferences. Here are three "no-brainer" tips to get the most value from any and all conferences.

Tip No. 1: Develop a strong preconference plan or strategy.
• Do background research on past conferences to determine which sessions and receptions might include the best prospects for new clients or strategic partners you would like to meet.
• Have a thorough review of the guest list, if you can obtain it in advance, to understand the background of the attendees. Review the list and place a check next to the people you most want to meet.
• Arrange pre-event meetings (breakfast, lunch or drinks) with some of the prospective attendees. Reach out by telephone or e-mail to schedule these meetings so you'll have a context in place before the event.
• Have discussions with peers, colleagues and friends who've attended the same (or a similar) conference in the past to get the inside scoop on the opportunities available.
• Organize a conversation with the event organizer to get more information about the meeting and to arrange introductions when attending. This can pay big dividends if

that person is open to helping you connect at the conference.

• Set goals for the number of contacts you plan to meet each day. Be aggressive with your numbers to ensure you'll meet enough people with whom you'll actually want to follow up after the event.

• Have a completed and well-studied infomercial or elevator pitch to ensure you're seen as focused and polished.

• Use a list of relationship-building and business-focused questions to ask those you meet.

• Practice role-playing to ensure you're ready to ask effective questions that can lead to the development of strong relationships.

Tip No. 2: Be sure to execute your plan at the event.
Thorough planning before the conference matters, but just as important is the next element — execution. When conference day arrives, you'll want to avoid becoming a wallflower or shrinking violet. No matter how introverted you might be, it's critical that you show up and perform with energy.

Advance preparation makes this level of interaction more comfortable and natural. Luckily, there are several tips you can implement to increase your "performance" at any conference.

When meeting someone new, try to be the first to ask questions. In the beginning, you should focus on listening to your contact and learning more about this individual. The more quickly you take in meaningful data, the more quickly you can determine whether this person is someone you want to invest more time with or if you would be better served by moving on and meeting others.

At some point during your conversation it might be appropriate to ask your new contact if any of his or her colleagues at the conference might benefit from meeting you.

Sometimes the person you're talking to may be better suited to connect you to a prospect than to become an actual prospect. Try to understand your contact's business role, position level and circle of influence. These factors can prompt the contact to effectively introduce you to his or her contacts.

In addition, your contact may know about a cocktail reception or other similar event that could put you in a room of possible prospects that you never would have met otherwise. Be open to connections this contact can facilitate.

Don't let a good contact slip away. If you meet someone who strikes you as interesting, well connected or a prospective client, be sure to get his or her card.

Try to make arrangements with this person later. You could do so by saying, "It was really nice meeting you and hearing about all that you do. If you're open to it, I'd really like to meet again and discuss ways we might be able to help one another. How about breakfast tomorrow?"

If the individual isn't available, make sure you collect all of the person's contact information so you can follow up accordingly.

Schedule as many quality meetings with other attendees as possible. You're not building your book of business when you're in your hotel room watching bad movies. Review the one to three days that you're there and commit any free time to holding more one-on-one meetings.

Just as when attending any networking event, label your collected business cards with A, B or C to ensure that you remember whom you met that you thought might be most valuable to your network. This also will help ensure follow-up with the A's and B's directly after the conference.

Connect with your new friends on LinkedIn. This will help you better understand each new contact's background and who else they know. This little step can make your follow-up meetings even more interesting.

Schedule follow-up calls with attendees before you leave the conference. If you're speaking with someone and it makes sense to speak again, pull out your calendar and schedule the time while that contact is right in front of you. This is better than getting back to them when they might be too busy to take your call.

Speak to the people sitting next to you at each meal and workshop. Sometimes the best opportunities happen when you least expect it. You can easily double or triple your chances of meeting a valuable connection just by doing this one thing.

Tip No. 3: Seize your window of opportunity after the conference.

The third element of being successful at a conference happens after you leave. Remember that, when developing new business, you typically have a short, 48-hour window to follow up to get the best possible results. You'll need to start moving when you return to the office.

Some of my attorney clients will wait weeks before making follow-up phone calls. Don't leave to chance that your new contact has a good memory; you can lose the chance to make a connection with even those who do once they get back to their daily grind.

Additionally, communicating early is important because the conference's energy is still fresh for your prospects. If you're looking for one way to help make a follow-up call or e-mail stick, say the following to a valuable connection before leaving the conference, "I'd really like to follow up with you to continue this conversation. Is it best to reach you through e-mail or just to call?" This way you also ensure you'll be touching base using the contact's preferred manner of communication.

Success tactics for following up with potential strategic partners
• Review the person's LinkedIn profile to see your second-degree and his or her first-degree connections. This will help you better qualify possible introductions you might ask your new contact to make.
• Develop questions to better understand the individual's business, including your contact's target market. Try to think of connections you could foster for this new acquaintance. Always remember that networking is a two-way street.
• Ask questions to understand whether meeting face-to-face or by telephone to follow up makes more sense. Disqualifying potential contacts is just as important as qualifying them and doing so can conserve your valuable time.

• Set a "loose" agenda for your next meeting to ensure both parties will get value and walk away with concrete plans to help one another.

Success tactics for following up with prospective clients

• LinkedIn is an excellent tool for following up with new contacts. Look for common first-degree connections to determine connections you have in common. This helps with relationship building and finding natural affinities. Then you can reach out to your new friend with a personal message and invite him or her to a lunch, drinks or a follow-up call.

• Take a few minutes to develop rapport. It's fine to talk about the conference or acquaintances you may have in common with this person.

Hopefully, you jotted some quick notes about your new connections while still at the conference so that you have topics to chat about afterward that you can tie back to your initial conversation.

For example, compare notes with your contact about who you thought was the best conference speaker or which was the best reception you attended.

• When you get to the phone call, be alert for, and even gently probe for, any legal issues or problems with existing vendors your prospect might be having. Anytime someone shares this type of information with you, this is an opening for you to move forward and help the person improve the situation.

If you do identify problems you could ask what issues in particular are causing the contact and his or her company the most frustration. Make sure you know he or she is interested in discussing this with you before asking this question.

• Schedule a full meeting during this follow-up call. The goal isn't to close a sale, but rather to gain commitment to the next step: a full meeting.

• Try to understand whether your contact is a decision-maker for the company or newer counsel. If not the main decision-maker, ask subtle questions about the contact's business to find out who the decision-makers are.

• Set an agenda for your meeting. This will set up the meeting to accomplish both your goals and those of your contact.

Keep in mind that relationship building takes time. Unless your new contact has needs for your services, it might be months or years before the business comes your way. The good news is that with strong relationship building skills, questioning skills and follow-up, you have a much better chance of landing the business than if you did none of the above.

Like with any good story, there's a beginning, middle and end. Think of each conference the same way. There's planning, execution and follow-through needed to have a happy ending with your conferences.

I'm sure if you think back to the last conference you attended, you'll see a number of my suggestions would ultimately have filled the gaps that existed without any processes being utilized. Use these methodologies, and you'll experience a dramatic shift in your results, which is the name of the game.

CHAPTER 39

HOW TO GIVE YOURSELF A GIFT DURING THE HOLIDAYS: WHAT ABOUT A FEW CLIENTS?

When you think about the holidays, what runs through your head? Is it the department store music? Is it the rush to find that once in a lifetime deal? Or is it the end-of-the-year gut check gnawing away at your psyche, questioning whether you've made good use of your time this year in building your law practice?

In speaking and working with hundreds of attorneys, I've heard my share of holiday frustrations around managing one's time. Mostly it's misperceptions about the holidays, which I call the Santa Claus Blues. Even though the holidays may bring cheer to many, it brings nervousness and potential despair to the attorney looking for some year-end business. Some of the things I hear include:

• "Everyone is away on vacation, so no one will meet with me."

• "These holiday parties are all the same- a huge waste of time."

• "I'm too busy (with the shortened month) to develop new business."

While these statements might be true for you in the past, I'd like to offer some suggestions for improving your outlook this holiday season.

Steve's Holiday Tip No. 1: December is the perfect time to schedule meetings.

While many attorneys believe that everyone is away on vacation, the reality is that most are sticking around. American Automobile Association research suggests that only one-third of the U.S. population will travel far from home this holiday season. Most trips will be within 50 miles. This relates directly to my point that there are loads of opportunities to get in front of clients, strategic partners and friends this December to develop new business.

I would suggest making a short list of 10 to 15 people to call to set up a lunch or coffee meeting. Think about your best-connected relationships and write their names down. It will only take a few minutes. Once you have the list completed, open your calendar and schedule an hour this week to make these calls. Do yourself a favor and take 10 minutes to do this directly after reading my article.

In my experience, you will be able to schedule three or four meetings, while also leaving another 10 messages to people who will call you back later today or tomorrow. The goal here is to schedule five to 10 meetings in December that you normally wouldn't be scheduling. When properly executed, these meetings will open doors for upselling, cross-marketing and quality introductions to new clients.

Steve's Holiday Tip No. 2: Effectively work a holiday party.

While it might be fun to attend holiday parties for the food, drink and merriment, you may be missing opportunities to uncover new potential clients. This isn't to say that you need to be a shark circling its prey. Rather, you might think about three things to help make your time more useful during the party.

The first thing I recommend is communicating with the host the specific people you would like to meet while at the party. Simply call the host or person who invited you and ask, "While I'm at your party, who are some good people I should be sure to meet?"

Once she's given you a few names, follow it up with, "That's great. Would you mind walking me over to them during the party to introduce me personally?" Just a few extra steps can make the event more worthwhile.

The second suggestion would be to prepare a few good business questions to ask when meeting new people. This might take away the awkwardness of what you should and shouldn't say or help eliminate a lull in the conversation. As you know, people love talking about themselves. All you're doing is directing the conversation to better understand their business or personal life at a higher level. A few questions that I've used include:

- What type of business are you in?
- How did you get into it?
- What does the future hold for your industry?
- What are some of the challenges that you face on a day-to-day basis (my personal favorite)?

It's also a good idea to ask one of these questions, listen and then ask a deeper follow-up question. The point here is that by focusing on the other person first, you not only understand if he or she might be a good prospective client or strategic partner, but you might disqualify the person as someone you should move away from quickly. Moving someone into the "no" column can be just as valuable for your time as moving someone forward to a "yes."

My last suggestion is to follow up quickly with the people you've met. Again, we might be inclined to wait because of the holidays. However, there's nothing wrong with following up the next day and trying to schedule a meeting in December or early next year. By following up right away you show interest and good communication skills, and it's more likely that people will remember you.

In some cases, I've built rapport to the point where we scheduled an appointment on the spot for the following week. Both parties were open to taking out our phones and getting the meeting on the books. Sometimes you just need to make the suggestion.

Steve's Holiday Tip No. 3: A failure to plan is a plan to fail.

One of the best ways to utilize any downtime during the holiday season is to take stock of what happened this past year. Really look at your activities and the corresponding results. Then ask yourself the following questions:

• How many clients did I meet with this past year? Did I do anything to ensure client satisfaction or loyalty? Was I able to open dialogs with clients relating to upselling, cross-marketing or asking for introductions?

• Who were my best strategic partners and referral sources? What industries are they in? How did I give back to my best referral sources? What did I do to find more strategic partners this year?

• What did I do to obtain new business that worked and what didn't?

• What did I do this year to improve my business development skills?

• Do I have a written plan for next year?

Based on your answers you either have a Cheshire grin on your face, or you're beginning to perspire. If it's the latter, don't fret. It's only December and you can still make plans to improve things for next year.

One important element in planning for next year is developing a solid SWOT analysis. This is an old-school marketing acronym, but it still works well today. SWOT stands for one's internal strengths and weaknesses as well as their external opportunities and threats. We can break this down further by defining them and providing a few examples of each.

Strengths: What are your strengths as a person and as a legal practitioner? You are a socially charged person with a huge network; you have the uncanny ability to read people; you have written 10 articles on one legal subject, and no one knows it better.

Weaknesses: What are your weaknesses as a person or legal practitioner? You are highly introverted and shy; you are new to practicing law and don't have much experience; you are a generalist, and no one really knows what you do.

Opportunities: What opportunities are open to you in the marketplace? You are specializing in a new area of the law, such as medical marijuana; you see an opening in a networking group where you will be the only lawyer included; you have hundreds of clients and haven't tapped into cross-marketing yet.

Threats: What are the threats to you in the marketplace? You are a residential real estate attorney, and closings are all driven by the lowest rate; competition in your area is out of control: There are 100 attorneys for every deal; your firm's name is not well known.

Going through your SWOT analysis and asking yourself the tough questions can be a truly eye-opening experience. By being honest with yourself, you can realize what, why and how to improve yourself and your situation for next year.

Einstein said the definition of insanity is doing the same things over and over again and expecting a different result. Make the important changes and take responsibility for last year's successes and failures.

The key to having a successful year-end is to not sit on your hands and let the time pass. December can be a very productive month if you focus on planning and setting some quality meetings — with quality people.

CHAPTER 40

REVISITING LINKEDIN AS A POWER TOOL FOR LEGAL NETWORKING

It's hard to believe that I started teaching LinkedIn over 12 years ago. Back then, in a room full of 50 people, I would ask, "How many of you are on LinkedIn?" Maybe 10 or 15 hands would go up. Today it's well over 95%.

However, it's my second question to a group at the CBA recently that raised my concerns. The question was, "How many of you that are on LinkedIn are getting value or business from using it?" Only one or two hands went up. Ugh...

The reality is that social media can be a massive time-suck and most people are pretty fed up with the negativity or the grandstanding that occurs on these various sites. The goal of my article today is to help you find value and, yes, even business, in using LinkedIn by cutting to the bone what really matters most. I'll break it down into four parts.

Part 1: Making the most of your profile.
So, you're in the process of researching kitchen remodeling companies and a friend refers you to Kitchens-Kitchens-Kitchens. You visit their website to look at some samples and the page says, "under construction." If you're like me, it's game over for Kitchens x 3! This may be what happens when a legal prospect comes to your LinkedIn page and finds no picture, phone number or well-written bio. If

you're going to have any type of online presence, put some time and thought into it. The best profiles always have:

o   A professional photo
o   A well-written bio that tells your story or business
o   Contact information to make conversions happen
o   A complete and accurate history of your successful career
o   Recommendations from clients if you can get them. People like to see others that have had success working with you.

Part 2: Getting the "right" connections for you.
This question comes up all the time, "Who should I be connecting with?" The answer may depend on what you're trying to accomplish. For me, I'm looking to connect with clients, strategic partners, centers of influence and attorneys who may appreciate my content.

My connection list is already at 7,600 and growing daily. For you it may be much less, based on who you feel would be valuable to connect with. The main reason for growing a larger list of contacts is to increase your 2nd degree connections for proactive lead generation. I'll touch on this in part four of my article.

The other reason is to increase connectivity with others so you can share your ideas, educational materials and to self-promote yourself on LinkedIn. If you're interested in growing your LinkedIn contact list, be sure to click the "My Network" tab at the top which will open up a page with instructions to import your computer or online database into LinkedIn all at once. This is recommended versus doing it manually.

Part 3: Posting content to get noticed.
If you're like me, you scroll through the LinkedIn posts that magically appear on your screen every day. You'll notice that some people seem to post way too much, while others are not seen at all. In my experience, the key is to be

somewhere in the middle. Additionally, I wouldn't suggest strictly doing self-promotions. People will get pretty sick of seeing how "great" you are and just tune you out. For balance, I do three posts a week. They consist of:

o   Educational material that I've produced (written or video) or sharing someone else's content with my own spin on it.

o   Promotional content that my contact may get value from seeing. For example, an upcoming CLE event where I'm speaking on business development best practices or an award won for doing good work in the legal field.

o   Ask a business question to get feedback and interaction. I just responded to one of these today asking, "Why don't attorneys ask their clients for referrals?" Good question, and I was happy to answer it and share my expertise.

Additionally, it's important to use images, hashtags and to tag relevant people in the post to get the best results. One way you know a post is successful is by the number of likes, comments and shares it gets. Overall, this is more of a marathon than a sprint.

Part 4: Using LinkedIn as a lead generator.
Now that you have a great profile, terrific contacts and regular content posted, it's time to get serious about what LinkedIn can really do for you! There are two primary ways to get leads, including:

o   Looking through your contacts' contacts. As you know, when you connect with someone, they become a 1st degree connection. This means that their clients, friends and business associates are now your 2nd degree connections. In most cases, you should have access to scrolling through and seeing who your clients know. For example, if my client "Bob" knows 37 lawyers in Chicago, I can write down a list of 10 that we could review together in order to identify who he knows best AND who might be open minded enough to speak with me.

o   You can type in a company's name in the search bar at the top and pull up all of their employees. Then, review the employees in positions of interest (GCs for example) to see who you know that knows them. For example, a GC at ABC Insurance shares five connections with you. Of the five, who do you know best that could introduce you to that GC?

At the end of the day, there is no better tool invented for business development lead generation than LinkedIn. It's all about learning how to use it and creating a comfortable approach to asking your best friends and clients to introduce you for the right reasons (to help connect two great people, for example).

To be clear, LinkedIn is not a fit for everyone. You need to be willing to invest time, money and energy into using it in order to get the proper return. I hope you have a better understanding of this diamond in the rough and can see some value in using it.

CHAPTER 41

ATTORNEYS NEED FORWARD PROGRESS WHEN BUILDING A BOOK OF BUSINESS

Imagine that you've just had a productive call with a new prospective client and she says, *"Terrific, let me think about this and I'll reach back to you in a few weeks."* You may not have been too ecstatic with that response.

Or how about your last 90-minute coffee meeting that ended with, *"Great, let's keep our eyes open for one another."* Have you ever asked yourself, whether such a networking meeting was really worth the sunk time and lost billable dollars?

One of the greatest challenges I see attorneys face daily is their inability to move business development opportunities forward to achieve a positive outcome. When I was coming up in my sales career, I always thought the worst possible thing I could hear was the word "no." In fact, most of my sales training back in the old days was centered around how to overcome the word "no" and turn it into a "yes!"

The reality in today's risk-adverse marketplace is that "no" may be the second-best answer you can receive. While this might sound strange to you, it's true! So, what do you think the worst responses are then? How about, "I'll think about it" or "I'll get back to you" or "let's keep our eyes open for one another." Aren't these the things you say when you don't want to say "yes" or be bothered moving forward? This is what buyers, like you and me, do to avoid being sold, coerced or convinced. Interesting, right?

That all being said, I'm sharing with you three tips that will help you to drive your business development initiatives forward to a positive conclusion.

Tip 1: Establish an agenda of truthfulness from the very beginning.

Anytime I meet with someone who is interested in networking with me or obtaining my services, I set the ground rules and get buy-in very early on in the process. This comes in the form of setting an agenda that creates a win-win outcome for both parties.

While I am not going to get into the specifics of agenda setting, here is one line that I routinely use to ensure success when meeting with someone new. Near the beginning of every meeting I just say, *"So ____, if we both feel that there's a fit for us to work together, let's establish a next step at the end of our meeting. Or, if we find it's not a good match, we should both feel comfortable letting the other know. Are you open to that?"*

The purpose of this approach is to set the table early that it's a "yes" or "no" relating to moving forward or not. In some instances, this approach actually takes the "think about it" routine off the table and allows the buyer to be more honest with you about next steps.

Additionally, it actually relaxes the buyer, in that you are giving her permission to say "no" if it's not a fit. As you may recall, "no" may be the second-best response you can hear. Getting to "no" saves you time, money and emotional energy because it's still moving things to a conclusion. Otherwise, the "think about its" can drag out engagements indefinitely, which is incredibly frustrating!

Tip 2: Set up the next step at the conclusion of the meeting.
If you've followed tip #1 above, you should now be positioned to establish a specific next step with the person you are meeting; this may be a second meeting, a return the subsequent week with a proposal or a follow-up call to provide referrals for one another. If a need has been established, and both parties are interested in continuing the process forward, you would simply respond, *"Based on our discussions so far, I believe there's a fit for us to work together. Let's schedule Wednesday at 9 am to meet again to discuss solutions to these issues. How does that sound?"*

While this is not a complicated approach, it's amazing how rarely attorneys set up a specific next step. Gaining commitment from someone to schedule more time is critical to understanding their interest and hopefully, their urgency to move things forward. Without this, a cat and mouse game may occur, which is an inefficient time spend and can chip away at your self-esteem. It never feels good when someone ghosts you in life or in business.

Tip 3: When all else fails, use email to get things done.
In some instances, people will make commitments and then just break them without giving it a second thought– especially buyers who are very busy or feel no urgency to take-action.

This is where a well-presented email may help. Here are two suggestions on follow-up emails to establish a next step or get back in the game when someone's being a little cagey.

Scenario #1. No next step was established at the end of a meeting. Here you must provide specific times/dates to get this next step locked down.

Hi _____,
Terrific meeting you last week. I hope you found the conversation beneficial. My apologies for not setting up a specific next step for us, as we discussed. How about a check-in call next week on Monday at 9 am, 10 am or 1 pm? Let me know which works for you and I'll set up a meeting invite for us.

Scenario #2. You've emailed her already and there was no response. We will remind her that it's safe to respond yes or no, to get some form of resolution.

Hi _____,
I hope the day finds you well. I emailed you last week and am checking back to see if you received the message. If so, it would behoove (or benefit) both of us to hear your thoughts about whether we should continue the discussion and move things forward. Or, if you believe there's no fit here, please feel free to share that as well. As we discussed, I am very open to feedback if you're thinking you'd rather go another direction. If you would like to speak again, I am available this Friday at 8 am, 9 am or 11 am. Please let me know which direction you'd like to proceed. Thanks!

This last email is interesting because you are coming across with some confidence that you don't need the business, even if you really do. The goal is to get you to the next step forward or to move the person to a "no" decision. You can then decide to address it or let it go.

As you can see, it's mission critical to set up the meeting for success at the very start, while also driving it forward upon its conclusion. Without a process to move qualified buyers and networkers forward, you could be wasting countless hours. I would encourage you to try these concepts and you'll see for yourself how positive things can be.

Part 4:
Practice Management

CHAPTER 42
IS PEER-TO-PEER ADVISORY FOR LAWYERS THE NEW "IT" FACTOR?

At some point over your legal career, you probably found a mentor, coach or advisor to help you navigate the legal landscape and to maneuver through rough waters.

Everyone knows that you can advance in your profession much more quickly with help, rather than on your own. In fact, I can't think of any successful person I know who can't point to someone in his or her life that wasn't the difference maker.

For me, it was my coach, Keith, back in the early 2000's. He was able to evaluate me as a business developer and identify my weaknesses and potential strengths like no one else. Within six months of working with him, I had locked up more business in less time than ever before. This experience led me to my true calling, helping ambitious attorneys rise to the top as skilled rainmakers.

Today, coaching and training on business development may not be a fit for everyone. For many executives, and now lawyers, there are peer-advisory groups that may be the wave of the future. My definition of "peer-advisory" is a collective of like-minded people who work together to share ideas, overcome challenges and provide accountability to accomplish their individual goals.

If you think about it, most lawyers feel stuck and alone as it relates to business development (even the rainmakers).

So, while it might be easy for lawyers to discuss case strategy or contract language, business development is rarely discussed.

I've had the great pleasure of running a number of attorney advisory groups over the past year and here are four unique benefits that are difference-makers for the attorneys who participate.

1. **Self-selection:** In my experience working with thousands of attorneys, we can go back to the old 80/20 rule. Only about 20% of private practicing attorneys are interested or actively working to grow business. When looking to start or join an advisory group, only the true business developers will show up. This self-selection makes building a group challenging due to the low numbers, but the lawyers who do rise to the surface will be ready to engage. It's like golfing with other passionate golfers or attending a rock concert with a bunch of raving fans. Everyone is interested and committed to being there together.

2. **Idea sharing:** What happens when you put 7-10 highly committed business developers in a room to share ideas on business development, marketing, organization and time management? It's pure magic! It is so refreshing to watch the interaction between my members contributing ideas, sharing experiences and providing direct strategic advice to one another. They are answering critical questions like, "How do you get the most out of a social media post on LinkedIn?" Or "What's the best email structure to get a prospective client back who's ghosting you?" Or "How do I balance all of my work when trying to grow my book of business?" The collective wisdom and interest in helping one another is simply amazing.

3. **The HOT SEAT:** One of the best parts of a peer-advisory or mastermind group for attorneys is the use of the "hot seat." While the language might sound menacing, I assure you the premise creates peace-of-mind and pure value for the participant. Every month, a different attorney is on the hot seat sharing his or her most challenging issue (just one). We follow a model that allows the partaker to explain in detail the issue being faced. The group then asks numerous questions to ensure the problem is fully demarcated. We then share suggestions and direct advice for improvements for the member to consider. Finally, the participant will repeat the points that really hit home and commit to taking action by a determined date (again, accountability). The best part is that many of the members share common issues, so more than the hot seat participant gets value from the exercise.

4. **Accountability:** For many of my clients, this might be the best part of partaking in an advisory group of this nature. You have billable hour requirements for the year that you are accountable to meet. Where's the responsibility to achieve your business development or origination goals? If it's only within yourself, being accountable can be difficult. It's like losing weight or exercising without a partner. What if you had one or two lawyers who held you accountable to send out those BD emails, attend that networking event or make that extra post on LinkedIn each week? How would that change the game for you? These peer-to-peer arrangements are critical to getting habits built to achieve your goals.

There are many ways to take action if you're interested in leveraging these concepts. First, you can create your own group within your firm or outside of it with like-minded friends. Just find 3-5 other attorneys who are hungry for business like you are.

Second, look online and see if there's a group of lawyers or entrepreneurs that might have an existing group that you could join. It's going to be pay-to-play, but most good things are. Lastly, feel free to check out my programs specifically designed for lawyers at all levels on my website www.fretzin.com/programs. As you can see, peer-advisory isn't for everyone. But it's a terrific option for open-minded and motivated lawyers to generate support and gain control of one's legal career.

CHAPTER 43

INVESTING IN BUSINESS DEVELOPMENT — A LAW FIRM'S CONUNDRUM

When it comes to internal attorney growth, many law firms struggle to move the needle and help their senior associates and partners effectively grow their books of business.

Many firms invest millions of dollars a year developing teams of former attorneys and industry experts who truly desire to help their attorneys to get ahead, yet have little results to show from their investment. Why is this?

The easiest way to explain a firm's shortcomings around internal business development growth is to look at what it really takes to become a lawyer in the first place. Let me break it down for you.

As you know, to be a great lawyer you need to work hard as an undergrad and graduate with a solid GPA. Then you must excel in law school for three years, learn the theory of law and pass the bar. If that wasn't enough, it takes years of experience to truly learn the law and how it applies to one or more practice areas. While I'm not an attorney myself, we can all agree that this isn't easy and it doesn't happen without a serious commitment.

Now, what does it take to become an effective business developer? This may be the dirty little secret that law firm leaders do not want to hear. Becoming a rainmaker can take a similar effort and formal education as becoming a successful lawyer.

Really, though, why should it be different? My entire day, every day, is working with attorneys who have no business to speak of and also attorneys who have million-dollar books. What do they have in common? No formal education in business development.

It really isn't fair to assume that business development can be easily learned through trial and error. Imagine not going to law school and walking into a courtroom to try a case. That would be pretty crazy, right?

When time is money, making mistakes in business development can cost more than you would believe. One of my clients invested hundreds of hours a year into business development, never achieving the results that he desired.

He attended all the events and conferences, gave presentations all over the country and made enthusiastic pitches to prospective clients. All that, and the growth still wasn't there. Without a formal education and coaching, it's very difficult to become a great business developer.

Here are three suggestions to help law firms make better decisions on their business development initiatives:

Tip No. 1: Do your research
If you're looking for programming that gets results, ask your peers and search online to find the coaches, trainers and consultants that have gotten real results for their clients.

Results will not happen in a one-day retreat or seminar. Real results take time, energy and commitment to succeed.

Tip No. 2: Don't invest in everyone the same way
While you want to be supportive and help everyone, there should be levels established to provide assistance where it's appropriate. Before investing, consider the attorney's seniority, potential, interest and commitment when deciding what program to engage each attorney in.

For example, first-year attorneys need smaller programs that focus on networking and building relationships. More seasoned and coachable attorneys may need training and coaching that may be more intensive, sometimes ranging from six months to a year.

Time management, networking and selling legal services are all processes that can be learned over time. It might make sense to handpick some of your best and brightest and invest in them. They are the firm's future and when done properly, grooming these folks can be a better investment than bringing over a lateral.

Tip No. 3: Program development is critical to success
When searching out a resource for business development or developing a platform internally, the key to success can rest on the program's ability to provide structure for the attorneys selected into the program.

As you know already, winging it is not a process. Attorneys need specific steps to follow and appropriate language to use to obtain real results. There should be materials and a sound curriculum to accompany the coaching and training to running a professional program.

Whether you select an outside resource or build something internally, be sure to use processes that have been proven in the legal space and that are up to date with the current state of the legal marketplace.

The harsh reality is that it's the business of law, which means that business development education is now as fundamentally vital as being a great lawyer.

As you know, you can't practice the law without clients to work with. The good news is that business development training and coaching is becoming more available and relevant than ever before.

If you begin to think about it more as an advanced education or degree that is necessary for success, it may be easier pill to swallow.

CHAPTER 44

GETTING THE RIGHT LATERAL IS NOT EASY; DEVELOP A PLAN AND STICK WITH IT

It's no secret in the legal community that firms are investing huge sums to win over attorneys who own large books of business.

It's been a proven method of growth that corporations do every day to expand and dominate the marketplace. The math is simple. Find a lawyer or group of lawyers with millions in business and acquire the businesses they control.

Unfortunately, there are two substantial missteps that are occurring when choosing to add laterals to the firm's team.

Initially, firms struggle to identify, interview and select the best candidates that would "fit" neatly into the firm. And subsequently, there's no specific process to effectively onboard the laterals to ensure a successful transition.

When added together, many firms are bringing in the wrong people from the get-go or finding the right people but leaving them on their own to figure things out.

Either way, this is a huge investment that isn't paying off properly for the firm or the newly acquired attorney. While the solution can't be expressed fully in my column, I would like to share some thoughts from my 20-plus years in recruiting, business and sales.

Here are two critical tips that I know can change the game for everyone involved:

Create a process for interviewing that is proven.
When taking a case to trial, you probably have steps that you follow which have been proven effective for you in the past. You may have even learned these steps from a mentor or someone who knew the ropes before you did.

Interviewing is the same in many respects. There must be steps that are followed to obtain the greatest result for everyone involved. The firm's future and the attorney being sought after are both at risk here, so try these alternatives:

• Steal ideas and processes from the most successful people you know. This may include former managing partners, human resources directors and even the recruiters you may be using.

• Create a specific series of steps that guides the candidate through the interview process. Start with a resume and online review (LinkedIn, Facebook, etc.) and move things to a phone call. If that goes well, continue the process forward making each step more in-depth as you go.

• Use science to ensure your gut is on the right track. There are some very sophisticated assessments which will help you better understand the candidate's behaviors, personality, intelligence and social skills. Use these assessments as a way to disqualify attorneys that won't fit the job or culture within your firm.

• Create "telling questions" that are open-ended to get the most from the interview. Have two to three highly successful and experienced attorneys or executives conduct the interviews to get a variety of opinions on the candidate. Running an interview in an unstructured manner will lead to a poor hiring decision every time.

Set up a structured onboarding plan for new laterals.
While many firms think that they have this in place, they don't. I regularly hear stories of the million-dollar lateral that is brought in and then told, "Here's your office and your phone, let us know if you need anything else." What?!

Execution on an effective onboarding plan will make or break the huge investment that the firm has just made. It has multiple steps and layers that help ensure success for the attorney brought into the firm. This might include:
• Assigning one executive committee member to be responsible for the lateral. This person would invest time over the first 90 days introducing the new attorney around and making him comfortable with the team. This also helps get the cross-marketing efforts off the ground.
• Setting up a written plan for the onboarding and training process. Creating a predictable and manageable plan for the attorney makes a world of difference. Most attorneys thrive when structure is provided.
This plan would break down the first week, month and quarter of the attorney's time as it relates to internal and external activities. The worst feeling is when the lateral has been around for 90 days and nothing has been accomplished to integrate him into the firm.

• Most importantly, it is critical to assist the new lateral in bringing over and growing his book of business. If he has sold you on the million-dollar book, that must be realized for this to work for both parties. Be sure to find external or internal training and support to get your new attorney rocking in the right direction. Everyone loses when originations that are expected aren't realized.

If you do that math on just one broken lateral, the numbers can be staggering. This could be the million-dollar book that isn't realized, the recruiter's fees or the unbillable time that was invested and lost forever.

Whatever the case, creating an actual plan and process can save the day — and is the bottom line for firms that think more strategically than in the past.

CHAPTER 45

DARWINISM IN THE MARKETPLACE: WORKER BEES AND DREAMERS

What would Darwin say about an attorney's ability to survive in business today? Which species of lawyer will evolve and which will become extinct?

"Survival of the fittest" is a phrase relating to competition for survival or predominance. Currently, there are three species of attorneys competing for survival in the marketplace.

The first is the worker bee attorney. This class of attorney is a skilled professional who bills a tremendous number of hours and primarily assists the busier attorneys at the firm.

The second type is the rainmaker attorney. This is the big hitter who brings in the whales and drives business into the firm. Without this type of attorney, the mid-market and larger firms wouldn't exist. They are also difficult to replace when exiting the practice of law.

The last type of attorney is what I refer to as the "dreamer." This motivated class of attorney envisions becoming the rainmaker someday, but doesn't typically have the knowledge, skills or discipline to make the conversion.

While the worker bee's future is at risk based on the hours regularly handed off, the dreamer has the opportunity to not only survive but also thrive in growing a successful and prosperous practice. He or she sees the road ahead and understands that building a book of business is mission critical to a sustainable future.

So, who will survive or become extinct in a harsher and overly commoditized industry? The answers to these questions are being answered every day in the news as law firms break apart, merge and new law school graduates struggle to find jobs.

It has never been more obvious that the attorneys without books of business find themselves wondering what the future may hold.

There are a number of approaches that attorneys can use to ensure future security and freedom in their practice. Here are four solid strategies for any attorney aiming to thrive in a competitive marketplace:

Utilize your strongest relationships for introductions.
They say in business, "It's all about who you know." The truth today is a little more specific than that. It's really about "How you leverage the people you know."

Let's take a moment to look at the importance of leveraging existing clients and strategic partners to obtain more business. As I'm sure you recognize, there are no better avenues to drive new business than a referral from a happy client. That being said, many attorneys don't ask for referrals due to the fear of coming across pushy or salesy or desperate.

Mainly, this is what I call "head trash." The reality is that your client is probably happy to refer you, but just hasn't been asked. Most attorneys feel awkward asking for introductions primarily due to a lack of a proper process and appropriate language to get the desired response. While there may be some fear in leveraging these relationships, it is crucial to developing a bigger book of business.

The first step is to clearly identify your best referral sources and simply ask them to lunch, coffee or dinner. Be prepared to discuss ways in which you can add value for them to ensure this is not a one-way street.

A few examples of adding value for a client during this lunch would be to provide her or him with a quality introduction to someone that can add value to his or her business. This could be a potential client, vendor or consultant.

Another way to make it easier is to first help solve a problem that is unrelated to the law. For example, ask questions about her family or other interests she has.

You might find she's looking to remodel her home and needs a good contractor. If you know one, offer the name. Whether the contact is a client or a good strategic partner, invest time with him. In addition to building goodwill, you will have a better opportunity to obtain a referral or uncover an opportunity to cross-market. In times like these, you are always better off utilizing existing relationships to find the most qualified new ones.

Work to become a specialist.

Bar rules state that an attorney cannot call herself a "specialist." But when you are a true specialist, you won't need to label yourself as such. The market around you will handle that directly for you.

With more than 1.3 million attorneys in the United States, competition has never been fiercer. When survival is a factor in the marketplace, nothing compares to being well known and respected in a niche area of law. Take a moment and think about some of the attorneys you refer. In many cases, it's because something came across your desk and you knew the best person to hand it off to.

Many attorneys have shared concerns with me about focusing their practice and the possibility of missing opportunities that don't fall under their realm. The reality is that the short-term gain of staying a generalist will not outweigh the long-term benefit of becoming famous in one specific niche of the law or a specific industry.

There are two easy ways to find a niche that might work for you. First, think about the area of law that you have become really talented in. Second, think about something that you are very passionate about.

For example, a very talented estate planning attorney who also has a passion for charity could become successful working with non-profits. Or a health care attorney who truly cares about the elderly could focus in the eldercare law.

Take some time and research the industries or related niches where you have an interest. Try to better understand how many attorneys have a similar focus in that niche and how crowded the space may be in your particular locale.

Lawyers that are known for particular areas are memorable and become highly referable by their peers. By focusing and eventually leveraging the experience of working in a niche, attorneys can build a little empire by concentrating in one area.

Embrace technology

Take a moment and think about how far technology has taken us in the past 20 years. We have gone from fax machines and corded phones to memory sticks and smart phones in what seems like a blink of an eye. One of the best and most underutilized tools from the past 10 years is LinkedIn. Most attorneys I work with tell me, "I'm on there, but not really using it." While I understand that social media is scary and can be seen as a tremendous waste of time, there are some silver linings within the gray cloudy mass.

The truth is that most social media platforms are not right for most attorneys. However, LinkedIn may be the exception as it is widely known by its successful users as the best networking tool ever created. There are three key elements to being successful in leveraging this technology to your advantage.

First, you must develop a solid profile. People are watching you and you may not even realize it. Having a profile that is incomplete or inaccurate can hurt your image. It's similar to a resume that is riddled with typos. Invest 20 minutes and look at some creative and more elaborate LinkedIn profiles of your peers. Mimic what they are doing and update your profile until you reach 100 percent complete.

Second, develop an appropriate strategy for what you are trying to accomplish. If you aren't looking to meet or talk with anyone, don't set up a profile and stay off the site.

If you are looking to get out there and promote your expertise, connect with the people who can help you advance your interests.

If you're like me and want the world to see you, be more open to allowing a variety of new people to connect with you.

That being said, I don't want to connect with total strangers. Unless they write and tell me why connecting would be of value, I will usually not accept their request to connect.

The third and most important element of using LinkedIn is to use it to leverage your best connections to get quality introductions. The greatest benefit of this platform is being able to actually see who your connections know.

For example, let's say I have a client who has become a friend. I can go into her profile and pull up all of her connections. If there is one that seems like the perfect introduction for me, I could simply ask her what she thinks.

Based on her response, I would follow up and ask her to make a call on my behalf to her friend and introduce me. It's just that simple. I have been teaching LinkedIn for years, and it's been a proven winner for new lead generation for attorneys.

Find help
If you were to take a trip through Africa, from the bottom of the continent to the top, would you do that alone? How many people are able to become an expert at playing an instrument without a teacher? Business development is a learned skill.

If you fall into the dreamer category and want to build your book of business today, it should be mission critical that you ask for help. This might be a mentor internal to your firm or an ally in your marketing department.

Another option is to try to find an experienced lawyer outside of your firm who might be willing to invest some time in helping you develop some skills or a specialization.

One obvious choice is to research and select a coach or consultant who can help you grow your book. There are many qualified people that you can hire to assist you.

My only word of warning is to thoroughly research and vet the right person for you. Research him or her online and review recommendations on LinkedIn. Speak with his past clients to ensure he is driving results to the clients' book of business.

While there are many ways to improve your law practice during turbulent times, most people are moving along slowly, as if a car crash is holding up traffic. The idea behind Darwinism for the legal business is simple. The fittest will survive and the weakest will die. Try to utilize your relationships, become specialized and get whatever help you might need to ensure success.

CHAPTER 46

THE CLIENT LOYALTY MYTH IN LAW: IT'S JUST THAT

As a history buff, I love thinking about government, war and political change what discussing topics that are relevant in business today. In the Declaration of Independence, it states that "all men are created equal."

While this may apply to how we treat others with respect and dignity, we can choose to be more selective with whom we invest our valuable time with. For the purpose of running a successful law practice, all clients are not created equal. As a lawyer, a critical element to running a fruitful practice is managing your time in an efficient manner. How and where you invest your time can make all the difference.

Imagine that you're standing in front of an apple tree, which is loaded with fresh apples. Some of these apples are literally right in front of your face, while others are way up high in the tree. For the sake of efficiency, where do you select the apples? The lower apples may seem like an obvious choice, however many attorneys are still working entirely too hard climbing ladders reaching for those elevated apples. When discussing low hanging fruit with my attorney clients, I always start with a discussion of their existing clients. Our goal is to uncover opportunities, which will produce the highest possible value for the time invested.

As we all know, before you can begin selecting apples you must first plant the seeds and water the trees. As this relates to leveraging existing clients, there is a myth that must be eradicated first. The myth is simple: if you service your client properly, they will be loyal to you. If you believe this for even a moment, welcome back to the 80s! Times have changed and so must you in the way you manage your client relationships. Statistically, it's six times more work and energy to find a new client rather than to keep an existing one. That being said, we all have to step up our game to insure that client loyalty is developed with intent. One of the best ways to accomplish this is to develop a client retention and loyalty plan.

Before groaning at the idea of writing a plan, I assure you this shouldn't take more than an hour to accomplish and can make the difference between success and failure in maintaining and building your law practice. Here are the three important elements of a client retention and loyalty plan:

Step 1: Develop a list of your key clients and rank them as an "A, B or C" client. As I stated earlier, all clients are not created equal, so be careful in how you rate these folks. I suggest three qualifiers for determining what makes up an "A, B or C" client. Ask yourself questions about each client and BE HONEST.
- How good is my relationship?

- Is this a relationship that I can develop and expand?
- Are we friends socially or is our relationship more transactional in nature?
- Does she call me for general business advice or just about the deals?
- Have I helped my client in ways beyond providing legal advice?

Next, try to determine how much opportunity the client has to grow or how connected this client may be.

- Does she have a solid network of decision makers that she can introduce me to?
- Is her company growing and expanding?
- Are there opportunities to cross-market and share work with my partners?

The last factor in determining who to invest the most time with relates directly to the amount each client has invested with you and your like or dislike of this client.

- Does this client invest a significant amount of dollars with you or did they invest almost nothing a few years ago?
- Was this client a complete nightmare to deal with?
- Did the client cost my firm money due to poor follow-through?
- Did the client continually question and argue my rate?

Based on these three factors and any others that you believe to be important, invest 20 minutes to create a master list of your top A, B and C clients so that you can move on with step two of this plan.

Step 2: What you are going to do here is to develop a list of contact and relationship building points to help ensure that we are investing the right amount of time with the right clients. Based on their ranking, you are going to do more for the high ranked clients and less for the lower ranked clients. To be clear, if you have a "B" that you want to make an "A" then be sure to increase the amount of touch points with that specific client. Here are a few examples of different touch points that you can use to develop stronger and stickier relationships:

• Schedule a lunch or coffee meeting with your client.

• Go out for drinks and get to know one another better.

• Send a card on her birthday and for the holidays.

• Take your client to a game or concert. (It's important to know what she's into.)

• Call your client to see how you can help her business.

• Email or call your client to congratulate her on something she's accomplished (business or personally).

• Email your client with an article that is relevant to her business. (You can use RSS feeds for this. Look it up.)

• Invite your client to a firm event or another high level networking event.

• Be a resource for your client. Find her a new vendor, strategic partner or an actual new client.

Use these ideas as a guideline to create your "A" column, where a number of these type activities would be used. The "B's" would receive less contact and the "C's" less again. For example, you might want to have lunch with your "A" clients four times a year, call each one monthly, email each one monthly and find a solid contact for her twice a year. Again, the "B" clients would get less of your attention and time, unless you want to make that client an "A-lister."

These are just a few of the many things you can do to stay in constant contact and help ensure longevity with your clients. The side effect of this activity will be to open up more doors for additional business and much needed referrals. The stronger the relationship becomes, the less likely it is that a client will leave over price and the more open to referrals she will become.

Step 3: Scheduling time to execute on your plan is paramount to your success. While it's great to set up a plan like this, it's not worth the paper it's written on if you don't implement it. My best suggestion here is to find 30 to 60 minutes a week and schedule time as "client loyalty and development time."

Without making the time and setting it aside it will never happen for you. There will always be work and distractions keeping you from this important task. Look at your calendar and find a spot weekly where you are least likely to be distracted or busy. You can even do some of this work on the train, in the evenings or on the weekends.

Choosing between retaining and developing relationships that already exist and have high potential for growth OR attending local networking events to essentially meet groups of strangers, which is a better use of your valuable time? There may be value in both activities, investing time with people who already know, like and trust you will typically bear fruit much more quickly.

CHAPTER 47

GOING SOLO: FIVE IMPORTANT STEPS TO ENSURE SUCCESS

Whether you're dealing with slashed hours, compensation reduction or general reduction in legal staff, it's never a bad idea to get prepared for going solo.

The unfortunate truth is that recruiters are only looking for "portable" books of business (clients that come with you) to sell you into different law firms. The minimum that I'm hearing now is $300,000! If you are currently a service partner, you are at risk.

If you find that the only alternative is to go solo, here are five important steps to follow to make the transition easier.

Step #1: Develop a game plan

One of my mantras is ready, aim, fire. This means that you must have a written plan before jumping into action. This plan may only take you a few hours to create but will save you a lot of time and frustration later on. There are three elements to this plan:

Objective: What are you trying to achieve?
Strategies: What are the two to three activities that will make the objective a reality?
Tactics: What actions do you need to execute on to achieve the strategies?

For a sample plan or to discuss planning with me, please email me at steve@fretzin.com.

Step #2: Identify key business resources
Make a list of all the resources you have at your firm or that
you might need going out on your own. This might include
database/bookkeeping software like Practice Panther,
virtual office space like Amata Law Centers, an office
supplies list, or even a business coach like me to advise you.
Speak to a few of your solo friends to ask for resources that
have been vetted so you can make better decisions and
waste less time.

Step #3: Get your brand established
While you don't need to immediately come up with a fancy
business name, you should look at getting your branding
established right away. This might include obtaining your
own website URL (website address), setting up your free
Google listing, getting your name/contact information set
up in all the legal directories and rewriting your LinkedIn
profile (with a new professional headshot). Don't overthink
these things, just knock them out so you can set up for step
#4.

Step #4: Begin networking
Now that you have resources and contact lists created, it's
time to go to market. Your best connections need to know a
few things from you in order to be helpful. You must share
your intent related to the targets that you need to get in
front of. These would include:
•   Prospective clients: These are direct businesspeople
that you want to work with. Details you need to share with
your contacts may include Persons positions/titles, typical
business size, industries, location and the types of
challenges that you solve.
•   Strategic partners: These are the people who are most
likely to refer you. If you are an estate planning attorney, for
example, you'd want to meet Real Estate Attorneys, CPAs

and Wealth Managers. Your contacts need to know this in order to move you along to these strategic partners.

• Centers of Influence: These are the most connected people around. They are the movers and shakers who may be able to connect you.

If you fail to accomplish this part, you may hear things like, "Let me think about it" or "I'll keep my eyes open." No good. Try to help your contact/friend to come up with specific names of people and then walk them through how to make the best introduction possible.

Step #5: Develop some fast business
One of the most important parts of going solo is to obtain success early on. This not only helps with cash flow but enhances your confidence that you're going to be okay. Work with your best contacts to ask for the business or the introduction, not because you're desperate for some work, but rather because you're damn good at what you do! Follow step four to meet with your best contacts, get specific names from them, and follow up to get high-level quality introductions.

CHAPTER 48

HARROWING LIFE AND DEATH EVENT NOT NEEDED TO SET GOALS

I'm sure you have read about people who were given a second chance at life? Well, I'm one of those people.

In 1996, I was a passenger on a privately rented plane heading back from Eagle River, Wis. Without much warning, the engine failed, and we started falling from the sky — fast! Before any of us knew exactly what was happening, our plane crash-landed upside down at 75 mph into a house in far northwest suburban Crystal Lake. I nearly lost my life.

For months afterward, I was a human pretzel unable to move or have any maneuverability myself. I had two broken arms and was helpless in a wheelchair. I doubted whether I would ever be able to do the things I had done before, to enjoy the life I had known. While working hard to regain my strength, I had a great deal of time to think. I never considered myself to be a spiritual person, but I realized the unimaginable gift I had been given. Surviving the crash that day, I vowed to do something meaningful with my life.

Learning and teaching business development and marketing had always been a passion of mine. In 2004, I started my own business with an emphasis on helping entrepreneurial professionals to grow a thriving business. The secret sauce was in my credo, "You get what you want out of life, by helping enough others to get what they want."

So, I set out to be the best business coach, trainer and adviser I could be. The goal, to help attorneys to get over the finish line with a solid book of business they could rely on through good times and bad.

As an attorney, it's never been more important to drive your personal practice upward. The mindset that I suggest aligns well with my credo. You can build a bigger book, only by helping more people.

While many attorneys despise the thought of sales, marketing or business development, it is clearly the best way to help more people. As you know, you can't help people that have never heard or met you before.

To hammer this point home further, here are three suggestions to living your life to the fullest while leveraging your skills as an attorney.

• Invest in learning time management.

Time affects everything from the billable hour to being home for dinner, so why are you still struggling with it? Probably because it wasn't something you learned, like learning the law.

It's unfortunate because we often don't know what happened to our time and then we say things like, "The day must have gotten away from me." The truth is, without controlling your time, you may not be controlling your life. My recommendation is to schedule a few hours to dive into a book titled "Getting Things Done" by David Allen.

While you may not initially grasp 100% of what this book has to offer, it's very doable to pull out three to five tactical and actionable steps to improve your time management. For me, it was a game changer. I know it will be for you, too.

• Set goals and drive forward to achieve them.

The No. 1 reason why people fail is a failure to plan. Establishing business and life goals is not only for the "selling professionals" anymore. If you're looking to improve your lease on life, you have to own it every day. Here's an easy to follow way to develop a plan in under 75 minutes:

Step 1: Set the objective.

What are your goals for the year? This could be making more money, having more free time or finding a different firm to join. For example: "I will drive my originations to $200,000 this year."

Step 2: Outline the ways the objective can be met.

This might be reading Allen's book on time management, my books to learn business development or leveraging LinkedIn to find inroads to meet new people. For example, leverage my existing network to find new general counsel to meet with.

Step 3: Develop the tactics for success.

These are the action steps that you will take to achieve the strategies you've set for yourself. For example: Work on LinkedIn for 30 minutes each day to uncover two to three inside connections. I will do this between 8 a.m. and 8:30 a.m. each workday before answering emails and calls. I will track all progress on an Excel spreadsheet that I will have done by May 15.

As you can see, creating a simple plan like this is not complicated. Just follow the guidelines above and knock it out. Then, leave it on your desk or desktop to ensure it stays on the top of your mind. While I'm not suggesting that changing is easy, you may want to consider the short and long-term ramifications of doing nothing.

• Enjoy what you do.

Are you showing up to do a job every day or are you truly enjoying your career as an attorney? This is a very important question to answer honestly to yourself. If your answer is a "job" it might make sense to look at options to change your situation.

That doesn't necessarily mean leaving the firm or not practicing the law, but rather, identifying things that you do enjoy or might enjoy doing. For example, I do not enjoy managing people, but I love coaching. The difference is helping people explore options for improvement versus telling them what to do.

Review this list and think about whether you're in the right place, at the right time, with the right people, doing the right things:

• Think about the firm you're with. Big, small or solo?
• Think about the environment you are in. Fast or slow? Hostile or friendly?
• Think about the practice area you are in. Stressful, mundane or stimulating?
• Think about the types of people you help. Difficult, laid back or interesting? Big-shot executives or mom-and-pops?
• Think about the area you live in? Too cold? In Chicago, yes! Or, like me, you enjoy having all four seasons in one day.

Think about the power of controlling your time, setting goals to achieve and putting yourself in the best place with the best people. It shouldn't take a near-death experience to make positive changes in your life. You just need to commit yourself to eliminating the status quo and driving positive changes today.

CHAPTER 49

SPECIALIZATION: THE GOOD, BAD AND VERY GOOD

As you know, the Chicago area marketplace is swarming with attorneys looking for their next new client. Will it go to you or to someone who is well-recognized in the legal community as a specialist?

Becoming a "specialist" can be a scary proposition as your messaging and marketing efforts change to accommodate this new direction. The obvious fear is giving up some potential business by speaking and marketing openly about only your new focus.

While most of these fears are not grounded in reality, most generalists are worried about the possible loss that may occur when making the transition.

In working with hundreds of attorneys, we regularly discuss the ups and downs to becoming a specialist. If the timing is right and you are well-prepared, it might be the best way for you to stay relevant, while also growing your practice and obtaining additional financial security.

That being said, it's one thing to be "known" as a specialist versus "identifying oneself" as a specialist. It's always better to be considered an industry specialist and leader rather than having to advertise that information. In some states, calling yourself a "specialist" is not allowed. Be sure to stay in compliance within your state's or states' guidelines.

Take a moment and think about two of the most successful attorneys you know. Really, close your eyes for five seconds and get their names in your head. I would bet dollars to doughnuts that at least one of the names you thought of was someone who is a specialist. It should come as no surprise that an attorney who builds a reputation around being great at one thing is memorable to you.

The reality is that when you build a reputation in one industry, market or vertical, your practice can grow more quickly than you ever thought possible. Of course, a number of elements need to be in place before taking this leap. Here are a few things to think about before making the switch to becoming a specialist:

1. You need to be the best at what you do.

Whether you are a litigator or a labor and employment attorney, nothing is more important than being skilled at your craft. When thinking about specializing, be sure you have the baseline skills and experience to succeed in one particular area of the law.

It might make sense to get at least two to three clients under your belt in a particular area to test it out and see if specializing in one area makes sense for you.

Achieving notoriety as a specialist may take months or many years to achieve. The important thing is that you eat, sleep and breathe within the space that you've chosen.

A good example of this occurred when I was badly injured in a plane crash back in 1996. That's right, I survived a plane crash. During my recovery from looking like a human pretzel, my father, a now retired attorney, put me on the phone with Bob Clifford of Clifford Law Offices. He chose Bob Clifford because he is well-branded as the leader in aviation and personal-injury litigation. We didn't speak to any other law firms because who could possibly be better?

Being the best at what you do and building a strong reputation around that specialty can make obtaining new clients very easy. However, as you probably know, it takes real effort and conviction to build a specialized practice.

2. Choose the right industry or vertical that's a fit for you.

The easiest and most time effective way to develop a niche is to leverage the work you've already done in one particular area. It may make sense to target specific people, companies or issues that will allow you to draw out more work.

For example, if you've worked with textile manufacturers and enjoy the work, be sure to target other textile companies in your area. You can do a search on Google or LinkedIn to identify the people and companies to call on. Try to leverage your existing clients and strategic relationships to obtain introductions to these business owners if possible.

As an example, you could call up your client in the industry and say, "I know you've been happy with the work I've done for you over the past few years. I am looking to help others in the same area. Who are you friendly with in the textile industry that I should be speaking with as well?"

The key here is to develop a great relationship with your client to ensure that he/she is open to making these types of strategic introductions. Think about it this way. If you had the best dermatologist and someone had a nasty rash, wouldn't you feel great making the introduction?

Another easy way to find the right specialty for you is by asking yourself, "What am I truly passionate about?" If you care about something, it drives you to become more involved.

For example, one of my clients is passionate about animals and is now focusing on working with dog shelters and veterinarians. She joined the shelter's board and is routinely interacting with prospective clients for her practice. She is wowing them with her ability to solve problems and is routinely asked legal questions from the board members.

These inquiries turn into business meetings and eventually new business. She's doing all of this without working harder than before as the new originations roll in.

Finding a niche that you are passionate about can make your legal career much more meaningful and enjoyable. You will also have a greater chance of meeting prospective clients as you will be interacting with them on a more regular basis.

3. Find a space, where there is space.
Be aware of your market and niche and who else may already be there before committing to a specific specialty. While you may have vast experience in commercial real

estate for example, there may already be too many lawyers in that area to easily separate yourself from the pack.

Do your research and try to find a segment of real estate that isn't as fully saturated. It might also make sense to branch off into other areas of law to ensure you have your eggs in a few different baskets.

When the recession hit in 2008, many real estate lawyers were hit pretty hard. One of my clients saw this as an opportunity to study estate planning as a backup plan to real estate law. This ended up being a great fit as he was able to leverage his real estate clients and personal contacts to help set up estate plans for everyone he could. Now that real estate is back, he has doubled his book by focusing on both specialties.

By studying the competition, understanding the marketplace and the amount of business generated in a particular area or niche, you can better hedge your bets when selecting a specialty.

4. Look to the future.

A few years ago, I had the great pleasure of interviewing Jerry Maatman of Seyfarth Shaw LLP to learn a little more about his successful practice. One of the key elements to his amazing achievements as an attorney came from his thirst for knowledge within his area of labor and employment. He voraciously read everything he could to better understand what was coming down the pipe to see how he could leverage it to build his practice.

He described in his interview the 1992 legislation for the Americans with Disabilities Act and how he got ahead of the law to be seen as the premier expert on the subject. He effectively packaged a "survival guide" for companies to better deal with the changing laws and regularly spoke on the subject before anyone else.

By being a forward thinker, he locked in his success and was repeatedly hired as the expert on ADA law by some of the largest companies in the country.

Developing a specialization or niche can be a game changer for you as a practicing attorney. For those who are worried about missing other business opportunities because of specializing, who's to say you can't take on new business in other areas?

However, by focusing your outbound marketing on one thing, you'll have the opportunity to build your brand name much more quickly than staying a generalist.

If you do your research, pile up several strong clients and speak with "intent" about your area of focus, only good things will happen for you.

CHAPTER 50

FOR A FEMALE ATTORNEY TO SUCCEED, DEVELOP A PLAN AND THEN EXECUTE

The legal landscape is always evolving. In the not too distant past, the idea that a woman could or should make it rain or run her own firm was considered absurd. It was a "man's world," and women were merely allowed to be in it.

Well, today it's a very different story. We now have women managing sizeable firms, leading general counsel roles and bringing in more business than many men. So, what's changed, and how do women capitalize on this opportunity?

The first step is to look at the positive shifts in the legal landscape. In data found in a 2019 American Bar Association study and 2018 National Association of Women Lawyers report, we see some interesting trends.

• More women are entering the profession of law than ever before; 50% of of law school students are women and that percentage is rising.
• More women are in corporate "power roles" than ever before.
• Law firms are more interested in diversity and balance than in years past.
• Firms are more family friendly; 88% allow attorneys to work from home after family leave.

That being said, there's still a significant power gap between the men and women in the private sector:

• On average, women make 20% less than men.
• The majority of women are not in a leadership or equity roles at their firm (only 20%).
• 93% of top earners are men.
• Women face the work-family balance much more than men.

While women are trending in the right direction, there's tremendous opportunity for growth here. Developing your legal skills, personal brand and book of business are critical to becoming a powerhouse in the legal industry.

In my experience coaching dozens of women lawyers, the keys to success fall into three primary areas: developing a solid plan for growth and sustainability; getting out of your comfort zone; becoming a master of your time.

To make the transformation from worker bee to business development assassin and firm leader, here are three tips that have proven effective with the women I've helped grow their law practices.

Develop a plan that can't fail. Most attorneys are "winging it" and hoping that business comes from their efforts. The key is to develop a plan that cuts to the bone. As you know, wasting time is the same as wasting money. Every hour spent doing the wrong things, with the wrong people, the wrong way, will most certainly keep you from accomplishing your business goals.

A good step before writing a plan is to begin taking stock of your clients, referral sources and contacts. Always focus on the low-hanging fruit first. Here are my ranking of business opportunities, from easiest to hardest:

• Getting more business from your existing clients.
• Cross-marketing your clients with additional services.

• Obtaining quality introductions from your existing clients.
• Leveraging your strongest relationships for direct business opportunities or quality introductions.
• Developing strategic partnerships with good referral sources.
• Attending conferences where prospective clients and referral sources are.
• Attend or join local networking groups and associations to meet new referral sources or to develop new business.

Based on your business development experience and strength of your network, you may be able to work the top of the list. Others may have to begin from the bottom. Whatever the case, create a list of people to contact and set aside time every week to proactively reach out to meet with them. Get out of your comfort zone.

A few years ago, I had a female client who was struggling with a big problem. She was attending conferences and meeting with the highest-level general counsel in the country (good), but she was in the "friend" zone and didn't feel comfortable bringing up the topic of doing business (bad). Additionally, this had been going on for years (really bad). From a "time is money" and a lost opportunity cost perspective, this was devastating to her.

Developing a plan to reconnect with key clients and contacts is great, but without the right attitude and approach to business development, it might all be for naught. For me, the easiest way to get my head wrapped around this seemingly difficult issue is to consider that I'm the best at what I do. I derive this confidence based on my past successes and results with my clients. My success, therefore, drives me to want to help more attorneys to succeed.

For example, I know that when I work with an intelligent, motivated and coachable attorney, no one can get an attorney better results. Can you say that about your work as an attorney?

If you know you're great at what you do, it's easier for you to buy into the idea that your general counsel friends, neighborhood CEO or past law firm partner who went in-house would truly benefit from working with you. If this is not the case, keep working on your lawyering skills.

Once you have the belief in yourself, it's time to craft some language to make the "ask" without ego or pandering seem like second nature. For many female attorneys stuck in the friend zone, you should try saying, "You know Becky, I love meeting with you at these conferences and truly appreciate our friendship. I am curious as to why we've never discussed working together. Have you ever considered this?"

Or, "You know Becky, I love meeting with you at these conferences and truly appreciate our friendship. While I would never want to jeopardize our relationship, I know I would be of great value to you and your company. Would you be open to discussing a way for us to work together?"

OK, so what's the worst that could happen? If your friend has great reason why you can't work together, well, now you know, and you can move on. If your friend loves the idea, you will be kicking yourself for not bringing this up years ago.

One of the best things I've learned in business development is that knowing is always better than not knowing. Sounds simple, but most business developers live in hope that things will happen. To me, hoping is like dreaming. It rarely leads to clarity, assurance or real results. Become the master of your time.

In my experience, this is only achievable to the lucky or the women who master time management. Similar to business development, time management is a learned skill. In fact, I was incredibly disorganized when I first started my business more than 15 years ago. My desk was a disaster, I was always pushing important tasks off and I could never seem to get anything done on time.

After my first year, I realized that this wasn't sustainable and decided to begin studying the art of time management. After six months I had cleaned up my clutter, eliminated timewasting activities and crafted my week for efficiency. Here are three things I did that made all the difference.

For me, step one was cleaning up all of my messes. I went through my two offices and my emails to throw out, file or take action on everything in front of me. This purging took more than eight hours, but it felt like a thousand pounds had lifted off of my shoulders. Without doing this first, it would have been very challenging to continue my progress.

Once the purging was done, I looked at my workday in 15- minute increments to better understand what I did all day and what I needed to change or remove from my life. This exercise will blow your mind. We are distracted most of the day doing unproductive and menial tasks. Ask yourself:

• What should I be doing or not doing?
• Is this mission critical or something I need to put off?
• Am I doing this efficiently?
• Is this task below my pay scale?
• Is there someone else that can do this?
• Can this be done early, late or over the weekend?

The key here is to catalog your entire day to identify wasted time, poorly executed efforts and tasks that can be delegated. The result should be more hours opened for business development activities and family time.

Many of the women that I've worked with start out with the same concerns you might have about balancing a heavy workload, personal health and the needs of the family. In the end, their optimism, motivation to succeed, combined with excellent planning and execution won the day.

The good news for women in law is that things are getting better every year. While I'm not suggesting that any of this easy, nothing worth doing usually is.

CHAPTER 51

CRAZY TIMES. IS IT TIME TO RECESSION-PROOF YOUR LAW PRACTICE?

In 2008 my phone started ringing off the hook. Attorneys from all over Chicagoland were panicking due to reduced billable hours, lost jobs and the uncertainties of the worst recession in our lifetimes.

So, here we are ten years later and I'm feeling like Bill Murray from the movie Groundhog Day, watching history repeat itself all over again. I'm observing attorneys daily who continue to believe that business will continue as it is, doing little or nothing to recession-proof their job or existing law practice. In order to help, here are five simple steps to begin recession-proofing your law practice today.

Step #1, take stock of what you have. Really have! Ask yourself the following questions to see how you stack up for a recession:

- What were your originations last year?
- What percentage of your work is for your own clients versus your partners?
- What do you have in the pipeline for new business next year?

If you read these questions and said, "oh S*#%!" it's because you are not in a good place for sustainability in a recession. I hope you know by now that job security is based on your value to the business (yes, your law firm is a business).

A lack of originations, your own clients or a full pipeline will put you at serious risk. If clients leave the firm or reduce their legal spend, what are you really able to bill? To get yourself motivated to change and improve for the year, take stock of what you have. The greatest rainmakers are the ones who are motivated.

Ask yourself what would motivate you to put yourself out there to grow your book. Is it money, security for your family or having a portable book? Nothing gets done without motivation and a commitment to change.

Step #2, going after low-hanging fruit. As a lawyer coach, I understand better than anyone the time pressures attorneys face every day. Between billable hours, family time and sleeping, it's really amazing you've made it this far. That being said, if originations must become a part of your life, let's focus on the easiest stuff first. By easy, I don't mean that it's easy to get, but rather, some business development activity will show faster results than others. Here's my ranking of business opportunities from easiest to hardest.

Easy to hard:

- Getting more business from your existing clients.
- Cross-marketing your clients with additional services.
- Obtaining quality introductions from your existing clients.
- Leveraging your strongest relationships for direct business or quality introductions.
- Developing strategic partnerships with good referral sources
- Attending conferences where prospective clients and referral sources are.
- Local networking to meet new referral sources

Based on your experience doing business development and how large your network has become, you may be able to work the top of the list, while others may have to begin from the bottom. Whatever the case, it's mission critical to do something to move the needle. You can get many of the answers to "How to get started" by reading my blog at www.fretzin.com/blog.

Step #3, get educated and fast! While this might sound like a shameless plug to hire me as your coach, I promise it's not. Just do something to learn business development and marketing to ensure you aren't stagnant in your law practice. Here are three things you can do to learn these skills today!

Tap a more experienced business developer on the shoulder and ask for advice. While some of the more senior people may not know how to get it done in today's environment (no offence meant here), this could be an easy way to get on the right track.

Read, watch and listen. There are articles, books, blogs, videos and podcasts that are directly talking to you. Get on the Google train and start researching content to learn business development. Set a goal for yourself to read, watch and listen to one-to-two hours of content a week (yes, a week), in order to improve your effectiveness when doing business development.

Research and hire a coach today. Again, doesn't have to be me, just someone who understands legal and has a track record of success. This may be tough to find, but it's worth the investment of time, money (your own) and energy to build a book that allows you to control your own destiny.

I know you didn't get into law to become a "salesperson" and you don't have to. However, learning how to market your practice is currently the best way to ensure longevity in one's law practice.

Step #4, make a list. In step number two I shared a variety of ways to drive new business. One of the most important actions you can execute to ensure success is in creating an A, B and C list of your contacts. Statistically, we all have between 250 and 500 people that we know. It's of critical importance to scrub your Outlook, Gmail or LinkedIn connections to determine who is at the top or bottom of that list as it relates to direct business, or connectivity to direct business.

It also might help to clearly define what makes up an A, B or C relationship. For example, if your close friend is the GC of a large pharma company, she might be an "A." Or if you have a cousin who is in the IT security space and works with mid-market software companies, he might be a "B." Okay, here's one to make a point. Your hair dresser who does nothing but talk about how cheap people are, might be a "C" or even a "D!"

By taking an hour to pull up, review and define your list, you will now have some direction of who to call/email and why. Then commit Monday mornings to email or call two-to-five of these folks to schedule coffees, lunches or drinks to get your biz dev activity up.

Step #5, putting this all together. Listen, I know what I'm suggesting is hard, uncomfortable and not what you signed up for, but it is the current reality of things. One of the philosophies that I engage in with my own business and that of my attorney clients is something I call the three P's of success. My three P's could relate to an Olympic athlete, a top chef or a concert musician.

It answers the question, "How do I become really good at something?" If you've ever excelled at something yourself, chances are you used my three P's without calling it that.

PLAN- It is very difficult to be successful by merely "winging it." Having a plan that provides strategies and tactics to accomplish goals is mandatory for success in any endeavor one pursues. Business development is no different.

PROCESS- How about going into court without any idea what you're doing? Or creating a complex meal without a recipe? Not a good idea. It is super critical to learn processes for time management, networking and bringing in new business.

PERFORMANCE IMPROVEMENT- Here's where the rubber meets the road. You can plan and process all day, but never get better or make things easier. Learning from mistakes has always been the cornerstone of growth and success.

When engaging in business development, be sure to track your activity to easily identify your gaps and mistakes. You can then work to fix them and improve as you go. I once asked a salesperson, "how many years of experience she had in sales." She replied "ten." After evaluating her further, it was clear that she really had one year of experience ten times.

As you read this chapter, I implore you to schedule time to begin thinking about and executing on your book of business. While you might be a young associate at a big firm or a solo grinding it out on the street, there's no better time to recession proof your business. And make no mistake, it's really "YOU, Inc." Even under the cover of a law firm's name. Having your own book of business is the only real job security that exists.

ABOUT THE AUTHOR

Steve Fretzin is the President of FRETZIN, Inc., a legal business development and marketing company founded in 2004. He was driven into the legal industry during the recession of 2008 when attorneys began calling him for help. While not an attorney himself, Steve has worked with thousands of attorneys in most practice areas. Steve is 100% committed to his client's success and works diligently each day to ensure they are achieving their goals of financial and personal freedom.

In addition to publishing "Sales-Free Selling", "The Attorney's Networking Handbook" and "The Ambitious Attorney", Steve has been featured in Crain's, The Chicago Tribune, WGN radio, NBC news and is a regular monthly columnist for the Chicago Daily Law Bulletin.

Steve is also the creator and host of "Be That Lawyer", a weekly podcast in which he interviews top rainmakers, marketing experts and legal tech gurus to explain and present the best ways to improve processes and help break down complex ideas, into simple and digestible concepts.

In addition to enjoying free time with his wife Lisa and son Andrew, Steve loves to eat healthy food, travel and play platform tennis. (Look it up on YouTube!) Steve's mantras in life are to control what is controllable and to not be afraid of new experiences.

Made in the USA
Las Vegas, NV
27 November 2023